SENTENCE *Structure*

A Communicative Course
Using Story Squares

THOMAS SHEEHAN
American Language Institute
University of Toledo

PRENTICE HALL REGENTS
A VIACOM COMPANY
Upper Saddle River, New Jersey 07458

Library of Congress Cataloging-in-Publication Data

Sheehan, Thomas, 1950–

    Sentence structure : a communicative course using story squares / Thomas Sheehan
       p. cm.
    Includes index.
    ISBN 0-13-035510-0
    1. English language–Textbooks for foreign speakers. 2. English
language–Sentences–Problems, exercises, etc. Readers.
I. Title.
PE1128.S5285 1997
428.2'4–dc21

                                     96–36981
                                       CIP

Publisher: Mary Jane Peluso
Editor: Sheryl Olinsky
Development Editor: Margaret Grant

Production Supervision / Page Composition: Noël Vreeland Carter
Interior design: Paula Williams and Carey Davies
Manufacturing Manager: Ray Keating

Art Director: Merle Krumper
Cover Art: Richard Toglia
Cover Design: Tom Nery
Interior Art: Susan Spellman, Richard Toglia, and Arnie Ten
Electronic Art / Realia: Todd Ware, Marita Froimson, Don Kilcoyne, Carey Davies

PRENTICE HALL REGENTS
A VIACOM COMPANY

© 1997 by Prentice Hall Regents
Prentice Hall, Inc.
A Division of Simon & Schuster
Upper Saddle River, NJ 07458

Printed in the United States of America

10 9 8 7 6 5 4 3 2 1

ISBN 0-13-035510-0

Prentice Hall International (UK) Limited, London
Prentice Hall of Australia Pty. Limited, Sydney
Prentice Hall Canada, Inc., Toronto
Prentice Hall Hispanoamericana, S.A., Mexico
Prentice Hall of India Private Limited, New Delhi
Prentice Hall of Japan, Inc., Tokyo
Simon & Schuster Asia Pte. Ltd., Singapore
Editora Prentice Hall do Brasil, Ltda., Rio de Janeiro

Contents

All the characters in "A Whale of a Tale" are fictitious, and any resemblance to actual persons, living or dead, is purely coincidental.

Acknowledgments

I am grateful to many people for their inspiration and help in the development of this book. First, I would like to thank scores of students for using these materials in experimental form. Their feedback has been invaluable. For their feedback on the pilot version, I would like to thank Joan Holladay, Patrick Kennedy, and Deena Ohana of the American Language Institute at the University of Toledo. Helpful advice has also come from Susan English and Adelia Dannus. Denise Friend helped with proofreading and gave useful suggestions. Other kinds of support have been given by Carol Butler, Deborah Pierce, and Barbara Sayers.

I am especially grateful to Alexander Lipson for his Lipson boxes and to Phillip L. Knowles and Ruth A. Sasaki for their work with story squares. For their detailed analysis of sentence structures in *The Grammar Book: An ESL/EFL Teacher's Course*, I am indebted to Marianne Celce-Murcia and Diane Larson-Freeman. Another author to whom I am indebted is Penny Ur, who wrote *Grammar Practice Activities: A Practical Guide for Teachers*.

Prentice Hall Regents editor Nancy Leonhardt believed in the project. Terry TenBarge and Sheryl Olinsky gave administrative support. Reviewers Amanda Gillis-Furutaka, Kevin McClure, and Roger E. Winn-Bell Olsen gave helpful guidance. Artists Susan Spellman, Richard Toglia, and Arnie Ten produced wonderful drawings guided only by my descriptions and crude sketches. Paula Williams and Carey Davies developed the book's final design. Development editors Margaret Grant and Samuela Eckstat tightened up the manuscript. Copy editor Ros Herion Freese checked for consistency, and production editor Noël Vreeland Carter guided the manuscript through pages to publication. Thanks to all.

Two people went to a great deal of trouble to get me the picture of the Altair 8800 computer. Max Lockwood, who owns the machine (and used it to help him run his pharmacy for a number of years), and his son, James Lockwood, who took the picture, helped me out, not to receive anything in return, but just because they are nice people. Many thanks to both.

For her love and support during the writing—and for the suggestion of the King Arthur legend as the basis of a story square—it is impossible for me to adequately thank my wife, Peggy.

Photograghs

Page 32, the picture of the Altair 8800 is courtesy of James Lockwood. The picture of the Apple II is by the author.

Thomas Sheehan
Toledo, Ohio

Sentence Structure: A Communicative Course Using Story Squares is a rigorous, semester-long, high intermediate ESL course—with a twist. The twist is the stories. The basis for the course, they provide a context for the presentation and practice of sentence structures. In addition, they serve as a springboard to many interesting topics.

The Story Square

A story square[1] is a one-page illustration of major points in a story. This book has two story squares. The first, presented in Chapter 1, is a science-fiction thriller called "A Whale of a Tale." Chapters 2 through 7 are thematically related to it. The first hour or so of class time is spent learning the story. (Plot summaries and instructions for the presentation of a story square are in the Teacher's Guide.) Once learned, the story is shared knowledge, a clear context with limited vocabulary, through which sentence structures can be presented and practiced. Almost all the examples and many of the exercise items are related to the story in some way. In Chapter 8, students learn the second story, "Adventures at Camelot," which is based on the legend of King Arthur. The rest of the book is thematically related to it.

The stories and related topics lighten the tone of the sentence-structure class. Topics suggested by "A Whale of a Tale" include space travel, aliens, endangered species, evil geniuses, and computers. Topics suggested by "Adventures at Camelot" include chivalry, utopia, magic, and exotic sports like jousting.

The Organization of a Chapter

With the exception of Chapters 1 and 8, which present the story squares, each chapter is divided into lessons which generally consist of the following elements.

The presentation of a structure: This is done through exercises in which students analyze the target structure, through readings, or through examples. Presentation activities are often labeled **Read It!** or **Analyze It!** Structures are always presented through a context: the story itself or a reading on a topic suggested by the story.

Practice activities: These consist of fill-in-the-blank, transformation, matching, and other kinds of exercises, which help students manipulate the target structure. The content of many of the practice items is related to the story squares. These activities are labeled **Practice It!**

Open-ended, communicative activities: Students use the sentence structures creatively. They may interview each other, write a dialogue, or play a game. These activities are labeled **Use It!** and provide a bridge from the stories to the real world.

---

[1] Lipson boxes, the forerunner of story squares, were first developed by Alexander Lipson for use in Russian classes. In their book *Story Squares* (Winthrop, 1980), Phillip L. Knowles and Ruth A. Sasaki include Lipson boxes, which they call *fluency squares*, and story squares, but the use of the story squares in that book is quite different from their use here.

The study of English sentence structure will always be challenging. The stories and related topics in *Sentence Structure: A Communicative Course Using Story Squares* appeal to students and teachers alike and provide an attractive means for ESL students to pursue what might otherwise be, for many, a daunting task.

The Teacher's Guide

Teachers using this book must have the story square plots, which can be found in the Teacher's Guide. In addition, the Teacher's Guide includes:

1. Techniques for the presentation of the story squares.
2. Suggestions for the presentation and practice of sentence structures.
3. Guidelines for many of the activities throughout the book.
4. More in-depth discussion of some structure points than are found in the Students' Book.
5. Answer keys.
6. Correction symbols that encourage students to correct their own errors.

To the Student

This is a book about sentence structure. It's also a kind of story book with two stories. The first story, a science-fiction thriller, is in Chapter 1. The second story, a tale from English history, is in Chapter 8.

It's important for you to know the stories well because most of the examples and many of the activities in the book are related to them. The stories give you a clear context to help you understand the meaning of the sentence structures.

Chapter 1

A WHALE OF A TALE
LEARNING THE STORY

 Lesson 1

The Story

Activity 1 — Get the Background!

Look at the story square on page 2 and read this introduction.

Three aliens[1] are due to arrive on Earth in a few minutes. Two people are rushing to meet them. One is a scientist, Larry Williams, who is hoping to make friends with the aliens and develop interplanetary understanding.[2] The other is an evil genius,[3] Sarah MacSnee, who wants to make a deal with the aliens. Her goal is to control the Earth. Who will be the first human to meet a creature[4] from outer space? No one knows. But the result of this first contact could determine the future of humanity.[5]

In addition to Larry and Sarah, there are two other human characters[6] in "A Whale of a Tale."[7] Barry DeLong is a brilliant[8] young Coast Guard[9] officer, and Paula Osmond is an expert in both computers and sea mammals.[10] Finally, three aliens and an unknown number of whales are involved in the tale.

The pictures present some of the main points of the story, but many questions are unanswered. For example, there seems to be a mysterious relationship between the aliens and the whales. And what about Paula? Where is she, and what is she doing?

Your job is to get the answers to these and other questions. Your country is very interested in this first contact with beings from outer space, and you may have to make a report to your government.

Vocabulary

1   an alien: a being from outer space
2   interplanetary understanding: understanding between worlds
3   an evil genius: a very bad, very intelligent person
4   a creature: a living thing, usually a kind of animal
5   humanity: all people
6   a character: a person in a story
7   "Whale of a Tale:" The title "A Whale of a Tale" means a very big, or unbelievable, story.
8   brilliant: very intelligent
9   Coast Guard: a part of the U.S. military whose job is to protect the coasts
10   mammals: kinds of animals including people, dogs, dolphins, and mice

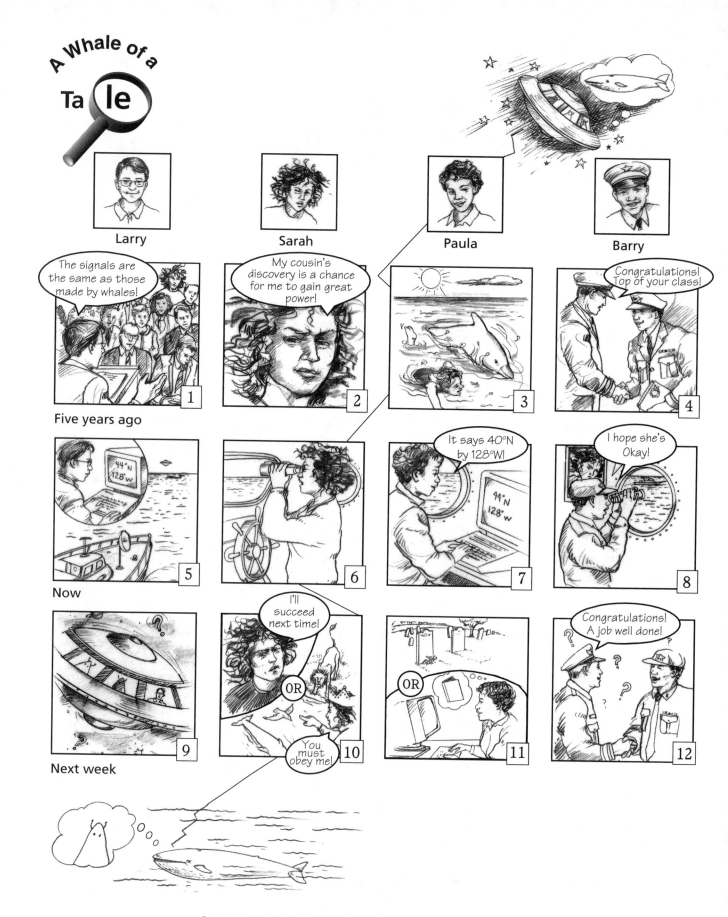

Activity 2   *Get More Facts!*

Read these major points about the story as you study the pictures.

Five years ago:

Picture 1: Larry gave a talk to a group of scientists about mysterious signals coming from outer space.

Picture 2: Sarah heard Larry's speech and realized that this was a great opportunity for her.

Picture 3: Paula, then a student, went swimming with some dolphins and became interested in all sea mammals.

Picture 4: Barry graduated at the top of his class from the Coast Guard Academy.

Now:

Picture 5: Larry is on a research ship cruising toward a certain location.

Picture 6: On her ship, Sarah is searching for something in the distance.

Picture 7: Paula is giving false information to someone.

Picture 8: Barry is looking at a ship in the distance.

Next week:

Picture 9: Larry may be traveling in space.

Picture 10: Sarah may be frustrated, or she may be the ruler of all Earth's animals.

Picture 11: Paula may be dead, or she may be writing a book about her experiences.

Picture 12: Barry may get a promotion.

Activity 3   *Discuss It!*

You have read some of the major points about the story, but there is still a lot you don't know. In small groups, discuss these questions.

1. Do you have any ideas about the links, or connections, between the characters?
2. What do you think you need to know to understand the story completely?

Activity 4   *Learn the Whole Story!*

Write one or two *yes/no* questions that you can ask your teacher to learn more about Larry, Sarah, Paula, and Barry—and the aliens and the whale! Ask your teacher your questions. Ask as many questions as you think you need to understand the story completely.

Examples:

Student 1:   *In Picture 8, is Barry looking at Larry's ship?*
Teacher: No, he isn't.

Student 2:   *Does Larry know Sarah?*
Teacher: Yes, he does.

Activity 5   *Double-Check It!*

Listen as your teacher reads each question. Then write the question and check (✔) the best answer.

Example:

Teacher: Why is Paula doing this dangerous job?

Students write: *Why is Paula doing this dangerous job?*

a. ☐ She loves danger.
b. ✔ She wants to protect the whales.
c. ☐ She's a computer expert.

1. _____

   a. ☐ Larry.   b. ☐ Sarah.   c. ☐ Whales.

2. _____

   _____

   a. ☐ It's not clear from the story.
   b. ☐ Radio.
   c. ☐ Telephone.

3. _____

   _____

   a. ☐ She is interested in studying whales.
   b. ☐ She hopes to make a deal with the aliens to gain more power.
   c. ☐ She wants to travel in space.

4. _____

_____

a. ☐ She wants to use them in the circus.
b. ☐ She loves animals.
c. ☐ She thinks she could then control people, too.

5. _____

a. ☐ 40 degrees North by 128 degrees West.
b. ☐ 44 degrees North by 128 degrees West.
c. ☐ 48 degrees North by 124 degrees West.

6. _____

a. ☐ Larry.   b. ☐ Sarah.   c. ☐ Barry.

7. _____

_____

a. ☐ Paula.   b. ☐ Sarah.   c. ☐ The ship he sees.

8. _____

a. ☐ Larry's.   b. ☐ The whale's.   c. ☐ Sarah's.

9. _____

a. ☐ Barry's ship might shoot at her ship.
b. ☐ It is unsafe to use computers on ships.
c. ☐ Sarah will be furious if she finds out that Paula is tricking her.

10. _____

a. ☐ He arranged the meeting between the aliens and the whales.
b. ☐ He planned "Project Alien" to trick Sarah.
c. ☐ He's a scientist.

Lesson 2

Your Goal in this Course

Activity 6   *Analyze It!*

The two paragraphs below are about two people who believe that they were abducted, or kid-napped, by creatures from another world. Read Paragraph 1 and discuss the questions on page 7. Then do the same for Paragraph 2.

Paragraph 1

The first well-known UFO[1] abduction occurred in 1961 in the White Mountains of New Hampshire. It involved Betty and Barney Hill. The Hills were driving late at night. They saw a moving light. The light came slowly near their car. They stopped by the side of the road to see better. The object flew quite low. They could see it. It was a craft[2] of unusual shape. Barney Hill used a pair of binoculars.[3] He was able to see some creatures inside. They were looking back at him through a row of windows. A moment or two later, the Hills' conscious memories[4] ended. Next, they were driving along the same road as before. They were slowly realizing something strange. They had "lost" two hours after seeing the light.

Adapted with permission of Random House, Inc. from
Intruders: The Incredible Visitations at Coply Woods, by Budd Hopkins, 1987.

Vocabulary

[1] a UFO: an unidentified flying object
[2] a craft: a ship or plane
[3] a pair of binoculars: an instrument for making faraway objects look near
[4] conscious memories: things that they could remember when awake. (Later the Hills remembered more under hypnosis.)

Questions on Paragraph 1

1. Do you believe Betty and Barney Hill's story?
2. If the story is true, why do you think the aliens were interested in the Hills?
3. If it is not true, what really happened to the Hills?
4. What about the two "missing" hours?
5. What can you say about the structure of the sentences in this paragraph?

Paragraph 2

The first well-known UFO abduction, which involved Betty and Barney Hill, occurred in 1961 in the White Mountains of New Hampshire. While the Hills were driving late at night, they saw a moving light that slowly came near their car. They stopped by the side of the road to see better. The object flew so low that they could see it quite well. It was a craft of unusual shape. With binoculars, Barney was able to see some creatures inside, who were looking back at him through a row of windows. A moment or two later, the Hills' conscious memories ended. The next thing they knew was that they were driving along the same road they had been on before. Slowly, they began to realize that they had "lost" two hours since they had seen the light.

Adapted with permission of Random House, Inc. from *Intruders: The Incredible Visitations at Coply Woods,* by Budd Hopkins, 1987.

Questions on Paragraph 2

1. What is the difference between Paragraph 1 and Paragraph 2?
2. Which paragraph seems more natural to you?
3. Which paragraph is written at a higher level?

Some international students say that the first paragraph is easier to read. However, the second paragraph is more natural for native readers of English. The reason is the greater variety of sentence structures. The first paragraph has only simple sentences, but the second one has many different kinds of sentences.

Your goal in this course is to learn how to write many different kinds of sentences. Your writing will become more like that of an educated native writer of English. In addition, your reading and listening comprehension will improve as you learn about sentence structure.

Activity 7   *Analyze It!*

Work in small groups. Select any reading, perhaps something that you are reading for another class. Copy from the reading at least five sentences that have different structures. The following examples might be found in an astronomy book.

Examples:

As the Earth moves around the sun, we see the stars from different angles.

The Earth and the moon, which are sometimes called a "double planet," exert strong gravitational pulls on each other.

Chapter 2

NOUN PHRASES
A REMINDER OF SOME BASICS

 Lesson 1

Nouns: The Basics

Activity 1   *Read It!*

Step 1: Elgin Ciampi is a photographer. During the filming of the movie *Flipper*, Mr. Ciampi met Mitzie, the dolphin that played Flipper in the movie. Later, Mr. Ciampi wrote about his experiences with Mitzie. Read the passage. (Starred words are illustrated.)

Swimming with a Dolphin

I took a deep breath[1] and dived into the clear blue water. Wearing my mask,* snorkel,* and flippers,* I went down fifteen feet to take a picture of her. She immediately saw my camera and came over to "buzz" it with her sonar.[2] She was too close for me to take a picture, so I gave her the camera, and she pushed it with her nose.

a diver with a mask, snorkel, and flippers

I ran out of breath and had to go up to the surface.[3] When I reached the top, I gasped[4] for air. A second later I saw Mitzie's head break the surface just a few feet in front of me, and I heard her also gasp for air. We were both mammals acting like fish. This gave me a feeling of being related to Mitzie, a feeling that I was to experience many times.

Vocabulary

[1] a deep breath: a lot of air
[2] sonar: a system of using sound to locate things under water
[3] the surface: the top of the water
[4] to gasp: to take a big breath very quickly

For months I spent many hours each day with Mitzie, and I quickly learned that she was happiest after eating. Then she seemed in love with life, and everybody was her friend. She would make a series of joyful leaps[5] out of the water, and then fall back on her belly,* making a big splash.* Often she would land on her head or on her tail. Sometimes she would swim on her back with her nose out of the water like a snorkel. When she did this, she really seemed to be enjoying herself.

Every time I watched her happy attitude, I wished that I could enjoy each moment of life and its simple pleasures as she did.

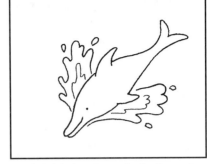

a dolphin lands on its belly and makes a splash

Adapted from *Those Other People, the Porpoises,* by Elgin Ciampi with permission of the author.

Step 2: Discuss these questions.

1. Why did Mr. Ciampi wear a snorkel?
2. What can a dolphin do with sonar?
3. Why did Mr. Ciampi have a "feeling of being related" to Mitzie?
4. In what way did Mr. Ciampi want to be like Mitzie?

Step 3: Make a list of at least fifteen nouns from the reading. The first three nouns are listed below as examples.

Examples:

breath   water   mask

Points to Remember: Three Groups of Nouns ·····················

1 There are three groups of nouns in English. The first group consists of nouns that are always countable.

a. a mask
b. a mammal
c. a picture
d. a flipper
e. a foot
f. a fish
g. a breath

You can count flippers: one flipper, two flippers.

2 Whenever you use a countable noun, you must make it singular or plural.

singular   plural
a. He wore his **mask** and **flippers**.

singular   plural
b. Mitzie made a **series** of joyful **leaps**.

Vocabulary

---
[5] a leap: a big jump

3 The second group consists of nouns that are almost always uncountable. (**Note:** Uncountable nouns have no plural form.)

a. water

b. sonar

c. air

d. news

4 The third group consists of nouns that are sometimes countable and sometimes uncountable.

a. **Countable:**   Barry has an exciting **life**.
b. **Uncountable:** Dolphins seem to enjoy **life**.
c. **Countable:**   Barry has not had many **loves**, but he knows he wants to marry Paula.
d. **Uncountable:** The dolphin seemed in **love** with life.

Activity 2   *Analyze It!*

Analyze the nouns in the passage by Mr. Ciampi on pages 8 and 9. Label all countable singular nouns *CS*, all countable plural nouns *CP*, and all uncountable nouns *U*.

Example:

                CS   U   CS   CS

I took a deep breath and dived into the clear blue water. Wearing my mask, snorkel,

        CP

and flippers, I went . . .

 **Lesson 2**

"Small Words" and Singular Countable Nouns

Points to Remember: Small Words Before Singular Countable Nouns · · · · · · · · · ·

① Singular countable nouns almost always have "small words"[1] before them. "Small words" are listed below.

Articles	**Possessives**	**Other Small Words**
a, an, the	my, your, his, her, our, their, its whose Barry's, Paula's, etc.	this, that one each every any[2] some[3]

a.   He took **a** deep breath.

b.   The dolphin pushed **Mr. Ciampi's** camera.

c.   Barry is not sure where **that** alien ship is from.

d.   Paula, **whose** fiancé is also her boss, is now in serious danger.

② *Exception:* Some countable singular nouns refer to activities, including meals. No "small word" is necessary before these words.

$$\text{Ø} = \text{no "small word"}$$

a.   **Ø** Basketball practice is at four.

b.   They are at **Ø** $\left\{ \begin{array}{l} \text{school.}[4] \\ \text{church.} \end{array} \right.$

Small words are sometimes possible, as in c. below.

c.   Barry has $\left\{ \begin{array}{l} \text{Ø} \\ \text{his} \end{array} \right\}$ $\left\{ \begin{array}{l} \textbf{breakfast} \\ \textbf{lunch} \\ \textbf{dinner} \end{array} \right\}$ with the other officers on his ship.

---

[1]   The traditional name for "small words" is *determiners*.

[2]   The following example illustrates the meaning of *any* before a singular noun: Larry said, "I need a computer, **any** computer!" This means that Larry did not have a particular computer in mind.

[3]   *Some* can be used before singular nouns in informal situations. For example, when Barry's father learned that his son was going to graduate at the top of his class, he said, "That Barry is **some** student." A more formal way to say this would be: "Barry is an excellent student."

[4]   The sentence: "The girls are at school." means that the girls are in class, studying. The sentence "The girls are at the school." means that they are at the school building, but it is not clear what they are doing there.

Activity 3   *Analyze It!*

Turn to Paragraph 1 of Activity 6 on page 6. Circle every singular noun and the small word before it. Draw a line connecting the two.

Example:

(The) first well-known UFO (abduction) occurred in 1961 in the White Mountains of

New Hampshire.

Points to Remember: More About *A, An, and The* ·····························

❶ The word *the* is used before one-of-a-kind singular nouns.

   a. An hour ago, the aliens were near **the** moon.

      (There's only one moon circling the Earth.)

   b. Larry told the scientists, "We will soon see a spaceship in **the** sky."

      (There is only one sky.)

❷ The word *the* is almost always used before ordinal numbers like *first, second,* and *third,* before the words *only, same,* and *last,* and before superlatives like *biggest* and *most dangerous.*

   a. The Earth is **the third** of the sun's nine planets.

   b. Sarah and Larry have **the same** grandparents.

   c. Sarah is one of **the most dangerous** people in the world.

❸ The "small words" *a* or *an* are used if a singular noun is new information. After that, *the* is used every time.

new
information

Larry made **an** important *discovery* five years ago. He told other scientists about

old   new   old
information   information   information

the *discovery* at **a** *meeting.* **The** *meeting* was attended by hundreds of scientists.

old
information

All of them were interested in **the** *discovery*.

Activity 4 *Practice It!*

The article on the next page appeared in a newspaper on the aliens' planet, Quarafanaflou, before the three astronauts, Smoch, Blurk, and Raltch, left for Earth. Unfortunately, the person who translated the story into English put almost all the nouns in the singular form and forgot almost all the "small words." Change each noun to the plural form if necessary. Label all countable singular nouns *CS*, all countable plural nouns *CP*, and all uncountable nouns *U*. Put a small word in each blank if necessary. Most of the time, you can use *a*, *an*, or *the*, but you will need other "small words" in a few blanks. If no small word is needed, write the symbol Ø, which means "no word." The beginning is done for you as an example.

Elders will send ship to blue planet

All want Smoch to navigate

1. There was __*a*__ long *meeting* in the Great Hall last

night. 2. All __*the*__ *elder*s attended. 3. At __*the*__

meeting, __*the*__ *elder*s had to make __*an*__ important

__Ø__ *decision*. 4. They had to decide whether or not to

send _____ *spaceship* to _____ blue _____ *planet* circling

_____ distant *star*. 5. Some felt that _____ *voyage* to

_____ blue *planet* was necessary. 6. Other _____ *elder*

became angry. 7. "Why can't we stay here and solve

_____ *problem* on our planet?" they asked.

8. In the end, however, it was decided: 9. _____ *ship*

with _____ *crew*[1] of three would make _____ long _____

journey[2] to _____ faraway blue *planet*. 10. Only one

navigator[3] on Quarafanaflou was able to steer _____ *ship*

on _____ such _____ *journey*: 11. Smoch was needed!

12. _____ great *navigator* Smoch! 13. He had been

in retirement for many _____ *year*. 14. His last journey

had been to the planet Yithrin to greet _____ *creature*

there. 15. Yithrin was very far away, and nobody had

thought _____ *ship* would return from _____ *trip*.

16. But Smoch was such a powerful navigator that _____

spaceship actually returned four years before it left!

17. _____ *crew* seemed healthier and younger than

when they had left—except Smoch. 18. Poor Smoch!

19. _____ *face* had become shinier with _____ *age*; _____

antennae[4] had grown longer with the strain of navigation.

20. The meeting with _____ *being* on Yithrin brought _____ great *happiness* to _____ Quarafanaflou, however, and Smoch became _____ *hero*.

Smoch
_____ great navigator

21. At _____ *time*, Smoch said that he would never travel in _____ *space* again.

22. Nevertheless, _____ *elder* decided yesterday that Smoch was _____ only *navigator* that could guide _____ *spaceship* safely to _____ distant blue _____ *planet* and back. 23. Somebody would have to visit him at _____ mountain *home*. 24. Klukuf, one of _____ youngest *elder*, volunteered to find him in _____ *mountain* and convince him to come out of _____ *retirement*.

Vocabulary

[1] a crew: the people (or other beings) that work on a ship or spacecraft
[2] a journey: a trip
[3] a navigator: the member of the crew that plans the route the craft will take
[4] antennae: (plural form of antenna) long feelers, like those on the heads of Earth's insects

Activity 5   *Use It!*

Imagine that you are one of the people in the story "A Whale of a Tale," or one of the aliens, or a whale! Write a letter from that person or being to anybody else. For example, you could imagine that you are Paula and write a love letter to Barry. Or you could imagine you are Larry and write a business letter to somebody in the government. Or you could imagine that you are Smoch and write a letter to a member of his family on his planet. Write between 200 and 250 words. When you finish, underline every small word. Label all countable singular nouns *CS*, all countable plural nouns *CP*, and all uncountable nouns *U*.

Example of a letter from Navigator Smoch to his daughter:

Dear Oork,

    I am sorry you cannot make <u>this</u> wonderful trip [CS] with me. Space [U] is full of wonders [CP]. The planets [CP] of <u>this</u> star [CS] are especially beautiful. I think <u>the</u> most wonderful planet [CS] is <u>the</u> one with many rings [CP]. Nothing we have ever. . .

(Smoch's letter continues.)

Love,

Dad

Chapter 3

SIMPLE SENTENCES

 Lesson 1

Clauses and Phrases

Points to Remember: Clauses and Phrases •••••••••••••••••••••••••••••••••••••••

❶ English sentences consist of clauses and phrases. A **clause** is a group of related words containing a subject and a verb. In the following examples, subjects are marked with *S* and verbs are marked with *V*.

        S   V

a. the whales are waiting for the aliens

           S   V

b. what the whales are going to do

         S   V

c. that whales are gentle beasts

          S   V

d. because a relationship exists between them

❷ A **phrase** is a group of related words that does not have both a subject and a verb.

a. have been communicating

b. very big

c. a very big ocean

d. in the deep, blue sea

e. having received messages from space

Activity 1   *Analyze It!*

Decide whether each group of words is a clause or a phrase.

Examples:

from outer space
phrase
that they were listening to
clause

1. a special ship
2. that they are receiving
3. she is looking
4. they want
5. through the binoculars

6. until the aliens arrive
7. although she was afraid
8. in spite of her fear
9. had been detected
10. why the aliens are coming here

Points to Remember: How Many Clauses in a Sentence? •

❶ Most sentences by professional writers have from one to four clauses.

    a. **One clause:**   The Hills were abducted and examined.

    b. **Two clauses:**   While the Hills were driving through the mountains, they were abducted and examined.

    c. **Three clauses:**   The article says that while the Hills were driving through the mountains, they were abducted and examined.

    d. **Four clauses:**   My friend read me an article that said that while the Hills were driving through the mountains, they were abducted and examined.

❷ A sentence with one clause is called a **simple sentence**. Sentences with more than one clause are called **compound** and **complex sentences**. You will be studying compound sentences in Chapter 4 and complex sentences in Chapters 6, 7, 9, 10, 11, and 12.

❸ In your compositions, most of your sentences should have one or two clauses. Some may have three. Almost none should have more than three. For your work in this chapter, which is about simple sentences, all your sentences must have one clause only.

Activity 2   *Analyze It!*

Work in small groups. Turn to Chapter 1, page 7, Paragraph 2. Decide how many clauses are in each sentence of the paragraph. The first sentence is done for you as an example.

> **Example:**
>
> The first well-known UFO abduction, which involved Betty and Barney Hill, occurred in 1961 in the White Mountains of New Hampshire.
>
> *This sentence has two clauses.*

 # Lesson 2

Simple Sentences: One Clause Only

Points to Remember ••

❶ Every simple sentence consists of one clause only. A simple sentence is made up of two parts: the **subject** and the **predicate**. It is helpful to identify the **complete subject**, the **simple subject**, the **complete predicate**, and the **simple verb**.

    a. Whales swim.

        Complete subject = *whales*   Simple subject = *whales*

        Predicate = *swim*   Simple verb = *swim*

    b. Some people in the military like to get as much power as possible.

        Complete subject = *some people in the military*

        Simple subject = *people*

        Predicate = *like to get as much power as possible*

        Simple verb = *like*

❷ When a verb is used as the subject of a sentence, it is usually in the *-ing* form.[1]

    Swimming with dolphins has made many people happy.

        Complete subject = *swimming with dolphins*

        Simple subject = *swimming*

        Predicate = *has made many people happy*

        Simple verb = *has made*

---

[1] When the -ing form is used as a subject or an object, it is called a gerund.

18

❸ In some simple sentences, two or more subjects share a predicate. This is called a **compound subject**.

Subject 1   Subject 2

a. **Betty** and **Barney** had a very bad experience.

——— Subject 1 ———   ——— Subject 2 ———

b. **Planning Project Alien** and **preparing his crew** were Barry's jobs.

❹ In other simple sentences, one subject may have more than one predicate. This is called a **compound predicate**.

Verb 1   Verb 2

Barry **studied** hard and **graduated** at the top of his class.

Activity 3   *Analyze It!*

Underline the complete subject once and the complete predicate twice. Box the simple subject and the simple verb. If there is more than one subject or more than one verb, number them.

Examples:

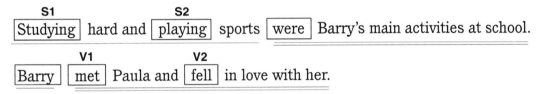

1. Smoch and his son said good-bye to each other.
2. Keeping the environment clean is one of Paula's passions.
3. Cooking and gardening can entertain Larry for hours.
4. Paula swam with a dolphin and had a great time.
5. Whales breathe air like people.

Points to Remember: Prepositional Phrases ••••••••••••••••••••••••••••••••

❶ Simple sentences are not always short. **Prepositional phrases** often make sentences longer. A prepositional phrase is a group of related words that begins with a preposition. A prepositional phrase can be in the subject or in the predicate.

Examples of prepositional phrases in the subject:

a. The woman **on the ship** is studying the computer screen.
b. The dolphin **with Paula** seemed to be a very gentle beast.

Examples of prepositional phrases in the predicate:

a. The woman is studying the information **on the screen**.
b. The ships are moving rapidly **to their destination**.

❷ Here are some common prepositions:

about	despite	into	to
across	down	of	under
after	during	off	until
against	for	on	up
at	from	out	upon
before	in	over	with
by	in spite of	through	without

❸ The simple subject and the simple verb of a sentence can never be inside a prepositional phrase.

Activity 4   *Analyze It!*

First, put parentheses around each prepositional phrase. Second, underline the complete subject once and the complete predicate twice. Finally, box and label the simple subject and the simple verb. (**Note:** Some sentences do not have prepositional phrases.)

Example:

The [woman] (at the computer) [is giving] false information (to someone).

 S — above woman, V — above is giving

1. Sarah is looking for something.

2. The aliens seem to have the ability to communicate with whales.

3. Barry and Paula will marry in the near future.

4. The young couple will marry by the end of next year and raise a family.

5. The beings in the spaceship may be related to whales in some way.

6. Computer crime is on the increase.

7. That restaurant serves brunch every Sunday.

8. The Amish people don't like to use much modern technology.

9. The batter returned to the dugout after his third strike.

10. It would be very difficult for anybody to survive for a long time without water in the Bad Lands of South Dakota.

Activity 5   *Practice It!*

Work in small groups. Add a different prepositional phrase from the list below to each sentence. Use the pictures to help you.

in the spaceship   ✓ on the horizon

next to Larry   by controlling all the animals

with binoculars   ✓ in Barry's hand

across the water   during Larry's talk

with a dolphin   without training

with the crown   over the horizon

Examples:

In picture four, the diploma is from the Coast Guard Academy.

In picture four, the diploma in Barry's hand is from the Coast Guard Academy.

The aliens have been in contact with the whale.

The aliens have been in contact with the whale on the horizon.

1. In picture five, the spaceship can be seen.
2. Larry's ship is speeding in picture five.
3. One woman left the auditorium.
4. Paula went swimming five years ago.
5. In picture nine, Larry is sitting.
6. In picture eight, the man is watching Sarah's boat.
7. In picture nine, the alien is over 1000 years old.
8. In picture ten, the woman is an evil genius.
9. It is difficult to use a computer.
10. Sarah hopes to control the world.

Activity 6   *Use It!*

Looking only at the story square, write two or three original simple sentences about each of the four characters in "A Whale of a Tale." Write a total of ten sentences. Include prepositional phrases in at least five of your sentences. Use your imagination.

Examples:

Sarah doesn't look like a very nice person.

Larry could have some real problems traveling in space with the aliens.

Activity 7   *Use It!*

Choose ten of the general topics below and write a believable simple sentence about each. Underline the complete subject once and the complete predicate twice. Box the simple subject and the simple verb. Include prepositional phrases in at least five of your sentences. Put parentheses around all prepositional phrases. (**Note:** It is not necessary to use the exact words given below in your sentence. They are general topics. See the example. The topic is "Larry's speech," but the word *speech* is not used in the sentence. If you want to use the word, you may, however.)

Example:

Larry's speech

   S   **V**
[Larry] [talked] *(about whales and aliens).*

Saturn

computers	space travel
Saturn	ships
dolphins	whales
the aliens in the story	spies
binoculars	movies
a genius (not Sarah)	hair
oceans	scientists

COMPOUND SENTENCES

 Lesson 1

Compound Sentences: The Basics

Points to Remember: Strong and Weak Clauses ·····················

1 In Chapter 3, you studied simple sentences. Every simple sentence consists of one **strong clause**.[1] A strong clause is a clause that can stand alone.

   a. Paula hopes to buy a computer of her own.
   b. Barry is watching a ship in the distance.
   c. Sarah doesn't see anything.

A strong clause can stand alone.

2 Some clauses are **weak clauses**.[2] Weak clauses are not complete sentences. They have both a subject and a predicate, but they cannot stand alone. They need strong clauses to support them.

   a. who are traveling in a spaceship
   b. when they arrive
   c. that the aliens come in peace

3 A **compound sentence** consists of two strong clauses. The two strong clauses can be connected with connectors like *and* and *but*, as in a. and b., or with a semicolon, as in c.

   a. Many people are afraid of the aliens, **but** they may be friendly.
   b. The aliens are approaching the water, **and** Smoch is getting excited.
   c. Some people are afraid of the aliens; others consider their arrival a great adventure.

A weak clause needs a strong clause to help it.

4 A compound sentence has **no** weak clauses.

---

[1] The traditional names for *strong clauses* are *independent clauses* and *main clauses*.
[2] The traditional names for *weak clauses* are *dependent clauses* and *subordinate clauses*.

Activity 1   *Analyze It!*

First, study each group of words. Write *yes* in the first column on the right if you think it is a clause or *no* if you don't. Second, decide whether or not you think it is a complete sentence *in written English.* Write *yes* or *no* in the second column on the right. Finally, in the last column on the right, write *strong* to the right of every *yes–yes.* Write *weak* to the right of every *yes–no.* Items with *no–no* are not clauses, so write nothing next to them.

Examples:

	Is it a clause?	Is it a sentence?	Type of clause
The aliens will arrive soon.	yes	yes	strong
The aliens in the spaceship.	no	no	
That the aliens will arrive soon.	yes	no	weak

	Is it a clause?	Is it a sentence?	Type of clause
1. Larry receives most information through his ears and eyes.			
2. The aliens get most of theirs through their antennae.			
3. Which are on their heads.			
4. Wants to travel into space.			
5. Sarah is an evil genius.			
6. Even though her parents were of average intelligence.			
7. When Sarah was a little girl.			
8. The other little children were afraid of her.			
9. Because she was very nasty.			
10. Nobody understood.			
11. Why she was so nasty.			
12. Paula is in danger.			
13. Barry is worried about her.			
14. Moving faster than light.			

 **Lesson 2**

Seven Connectors for Compound Sentences

Points to Remember: *And, But, Yet,* and *For* ···

❶ The connector[1] *and* means *in addition* or *also.*

Barry loves Paula, **and** Paula loves Barry.

❷ There is a comma before the connector in a compound sentence. (**Note:** Professional writers sometimes omit this comma, but students should always use it to avoid mistakes.)

Barry loves Paula, and Paula loves Barry.
                        ↖ **comma**

❸ *But* is used to connect two contrasting ideas.

Larry would like to have good relationships with all his cousins, **but** Sarah has no interest in friendship.

❹ *Yet* and *but* have similar meanings. *Yet* emphasizes the contrast between two ideas more than *but.* It means *in spite of this.*

Larry knows almost nothing about the aliens, **yet** he wants to travel to their planet.

❺ Do not confuse the connector *yet* with the adverb *yet.*

We know very little about the aliens because they haven't arrived **yet.**

❻ The meaning of the connector *for* is similar to the meaning of *because. Because* indicates a very direct cause and effect.

     ——— **effect** ———   ——— **cause** ———
a. People dislike Sarah **because** she is nasty.

The cause/effect relationship is less direct with *for.*

b. Larry must be careful, **for** little is known about the aliens.

---

[1] The traditional name for this kind of connector is *coordinating conjunction.*

Activity 2   *Practice It!*

In each group, match each sentence on the left with the one on the right that is about the same subject. Then combine each pair of sentences with *and, but* (or *yet*), or *for*. Use a different connector in each item of every group. Remember the comma.

Examples:

1. The computer screen says one thing.
2. The boy threw the newspaper.

a. It landed on the front porch.
b. Paula is telling Sarah another.

1. The computer screen says one thing, but Paula is telling Sarah another.

2. The boy threw the newspaper, and it landed on the front porch.

Group 1

1. My roommate turned off the stereo and the TV.
2. Roger doesn't know how to cook.
3. Barry is an intelligent man.

a. He will go far in the Coast Guard.
b. He has invited eight people to dinner.
c. He cannot study with any kind of noise.

Group 2

4. Paula had no interest in working for the ABC Company.
5. The crops did not grow.
6. Alexia did the laundry.

a. The rains did not come
b. She had a job interview there.
c. Her husband cleaned the kitchen.

Group 3

7. I told a joke.
8. Alyson works hard in her garden.
9. It will be hard to communicate with Smoch.
10. Ms. Barns saw a large craft with flashing lights coming down toward her from the sky.

a. Her flowers are beautiful.
b. Nobody laughed.
c. He knows no human language.
d. She continued eating her picnic lunch.

❶ *So* is the opposite of *because* and *for.* In cause/effect sentences, the cause follows the word *because*.

———————— **cause** ————————

   a. Paula must be very careful because Sarah will kill to achieve her goals.

The effect follows the connector *so*, however.

———————— **effect** ————————

   b. Sarah will kill to achieve her goals, **so** Paula must be very careful.

❷ *Or* indicates that there are two alternatives.

     The aliens may be warlike, **or** they may be peaceful.

❸ Compound sentences with *or* often begin with the word *either*. This word is not necessary.

OR

   a. **Correct:** **Either** Sarah will succeed, **or** the Coast Guard will succeed.

   b. **Correct:** Sarah will succeed, **or** the Coast Guard will succeed.

❹ We use *nor* to connect two negative ideas. After *nor*, you must put a helping verb[1] before the subject in the second clause. The second clause looks like a question, but it is not a question.

   a. Sarah doesn't know Paula's true identity, **nor does she** suspect her true goal.

   b. Smoch has not studied English, **nor has he** learned any other human language.

Activity 3   *Practice It!*

Combine each pair of sentences with *nor*. Remember to make the necessary grammatical changes.

   Example:

   Larry does not know the aliens' language. Smoch does not know any human language.

   Larry does not know the aliens' language, nor does Smoch know any human language.

   1. Larry does not like Sarah. Sarah does not like Larry.
   2. Whales cannot survive long out of water. They cannot stay indefinitely underwater without breathing.
   3. Paula did not study astronomy in college. She did not study French.
   4. Larry's research was not finished last month. It will not be finished next month.
   5. The aliens do not have a television. They do not want one.

[1] Helping verbs are called *auxiliary verbs* or *power words*. Examples: *do, are, can, had*, etc.

Activity 4   *Practice It!*

In each group, match each sentence on the left with the one on the right that is about the same subject. Then combine each pair of sentences with *so, or,* or *nor*. Use a different connector in each item of every group. Remember the comma. Make necessary grammatical changes with *nor*.

Examples:

1. Paula likes to swim with dolphins.
2. Young people in many countries do not choose their own spouses.

a. They do not get married without parental permission.
b. She swims with them as often as possible.

1. *Paula likes dolphins, so she swims with them as often as possible.*

2. *Young people in many countries do not choose their own spouses, nor do they get married without parental permission.*

Group 1

1. Betty and Barney Hill "lost" two hours one night.
2. Sarah had never been on a ship before last month.
3. Sarah will reach the aliens first.

a. Larry will make the first contact.
b. She had never traveled in an airplane.
c. They felt very confused.

Group 2

4. Kathy and Tricia want to run the Boston Marathon next year.
5. The Hills are crazy.
6. Some people do not believe reports about beings from other planets.

a. They do not want to hear any information about aliens.
b. They were really abducted by aliens.
c. They run twelve miles a day.

Group 3

7. My sister is a vegetarian.
8. Sarah will be pleased with her success next week.
9. Computers cannot think.

a. They cannot solve problems without instructions from people.
b. She will be planning her next evil project.
c. She eats no meat.

Group 4

10. Frank is interested in archaeology.
11. Blurk will remain on Earth.
12. Smoch did not want to travel to Earth.

a. He didn't plan to come out of retirement.
b. He is going to Mexico to see the Mayan ruins.
c. He will return to his planet.

Activity 5   *Use It!*

Write an original compound sentence with the words given. Make necessary grammatical changes with *nor*. Remember correct punctuation and capitalization. Your sentences must be believable. They may be about your life, or they may be about "A Whale of a Tale."

Examples:

sunny / so

The weather was sunny, so Paula had a wonderful time with the dolphin.

know / nor

I don't know the Canadian Prime Minister, nor does he know me.

1. hobby / so
2. money / for
3. tired / but
4. money / nor
5. married / nor

6. french fries / and
7. nervous / yet
8. aliens / or
9. funny / but
10. computer / but

Activity 6   *Use It!*

Choose five of the general topics below and interview a classmate about them. Then write five true compound sentences about your classmate, each one with a different connector, and each one on a different topic. Write the topic before each sentence. At least one sentence must include the connector *nor*. (**Note:** It is not necessary to use the exact words given. They are general topics. See the first example below. The topic is food, but the word *food* is not used in the sentence. If you want to use the word, you may, however.)

Examples:

food

food: Felicia loves chocolate, but she tries not to buy it too often.

furniture

furniture: Felicia saves money whenever possible, so she buys most of her furniture at garage sales.

sports

home

weekends

transportation

brothers and sisters

music

parties

pets

marriage

nature

Chapter 5

COMPARATIVES

 Lesson 1

A Look at Some Comparatives

Activity 1   *Read It!*

Small computers are so common today that it is hard to imagine a world without them. Before 1977, however, there were none. Computers were big, expensive machines. Read the story below about the Apple II, the first popular personal computer. Then answer the questions.

The First Personal Computers

The story of the first popular personal computer is the story of three men. The first was Stephen G. Wozniak. "Woz" was an electronics genius, and as a teenager in the 1960s, he built gadgets[1] as complicated as transistor radios. He read everything he could find about computers and knew more about them than his teachers did. He was less interested in other subjects, however, and he did poorly in school.

After high school, Woz attended two different colleges, quit, worked for a year at a small computer company, returned to school, and then worked for Hewlett-Packard.[2] He didn't need a degree to make good money.

In 1971, Woz met Steven P. Jobs, who, at 16, was five years younger than Woz. The two became good friends. Jobs was as bored with formal education as Woz had been. He was also interested in electronics, especially in a device[3] that allowed people to make free phone calls. Even though it was illegal to use this machine, the two produced and sold more than a hundred.

Jobs dropped out of[4] college before the end of his first year and started working nights on video games for the Atari company. As often as possible, Woz came to visit him and to play the games. Like Woz, Jobs was able to make a good living without a degree.

Vocabulary

---

[1]   a gadget: a small machine designed for a special use
[2]   Hewlett-Packard: a very large computer company
[3]   a device: a machine
[4]   to drop out of (school): to quit (school)

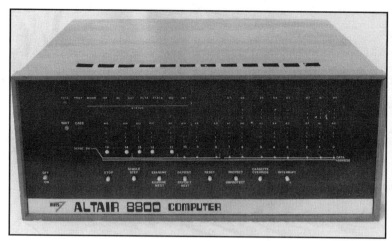

The Altair 8800 Computer   The Apple II Computer

At that time, an important event occurred in the history of computers. A company called MITS developed the Altair 8800 Computer. This machine was much smaller than any other computer. Unfortunately, it was difficult to program the Altair 8800 to do even the simplest jobs. Nevertheless, computer hobbyists were fascinated by it. Realizing that the biggest problem with the Altair 8800 was that it could not be easily programmed, Woz knew he could do better. He paid $20 for a 6502 microprocessor[5] and, over the next six months, he and Jobs created a version[6] of the BASIC computer language[7] for it. With the BASIC language, hobbyists could easily program a computer to play games and do useful jobs. Finally, Woz combined the microprocessor with some other parts to make a computer. Although Woz's machine was not as powerful as the Altair 8800, it could be built more cheaply and was less complicated to use. Hobbyists loved it.

Jobs and Woz sold everything they had and borrowed money from friends to start the Apple Computer Company. The two young men were able to sell 175 of their Apple I computers to hobbyists in the San Francisco area.

While Woz worked on a better machine, the Apple II, Jobs tried to raise more money. He met A. C. Markkula, a wealthy man in the computer business. Markkula believed that the Apple II would interest average people more than previous computers, so he raised about $1 million from various sources, and he helped Woz and Jobs to organize their business.

The Apple II came out in 1977. It was cheap, easy to program, and great for video games. Soon, Apple Computers was the fastest growing company in U.S. history, and Markkula, Woz, and Jobs all became multimillionaires.

Vocabulary

[5] a microprocessor: the electronic "brain" of a computer

[6] a version: a kind

[7] the BASIC computer language: Beginner's All-purpose Symbolic Instruction Code is a set of words and symbols that computer programmers can use to tell a computer what to do. Most computers have a BASIC language. The BASIC language is different for each microprocessor.

Answer these questions:

1. Why weren't Woz and Jobs interested in their classes at school?
2. What do you think about the young men's business in "phone call machines"?
3. What was the main problem with the Altair 8800?
4. Why was it important for a computer to have the BASIC language?
5. Who bought the Apple I?
6. Why was the Apple II successful?

Point to Remember: Some Comparative Structures ·····················

Here are some examples of comparative structures that you will be studying in this chapter.

a. as smart (as)

b. smarter (than)

c. more intelligent (than)

d. less intelligent (than)

e. like

f. different (from)

g. the smartest

h. the most intelligent

i. the least intelligent

Activity 2   *Study It!*

There are nineteen examples of comparative and superlative structures in the article on pages 31–32. The first two are given below. Find and underline the other seventeen.

Examples:

gadgets <u>as complicated as</u> transistor radios

knew <u>more</u> about them <u>than</u> his teachers did

 **Lesson 2**

Comparatives of Equality

Points to Remember: *As . . . As* ··

❶ Use *as* (adjective) *as* and *as* (adverb) *as* to show equality.

    a. **Adjective:** Barry is **as tall as** Larry.

                     (= Both Larry and Barry are
                      5 feet 11 inches tall.)

    b. **Adverb:**   Smoch calculates **as correctly as** the
                      Coast Guard computer.

❷ Auxiliary verbs are sometimes used at the end of
sentences with *as . . . as*, but they are not necessary.

    a. **Correct:**   Barry is as tall as Larry **is**.

    b. **Correct:**   Barry is as tall as Larry.

    c. **Correct:**   Smoch calculates as correctly as the Coast Guard computer **does**.

    d. **Correct:**   Smoch calculates as correctly as the Coast Guard computer.

❸ You may find variations on this structure.

    a. The people of the world are **as excited** about the arrival of the aliens **as** they were
about the end of World War II.

       (= People were very excited about the end of World War II. They are very excited
about the arrival of the aliens.)

    b. Calculus was **as interesting** for Barry **as** marine biology was for Paula.

       (= Calculus was very interesting for Barry. Marine biology was very interesting for
Paula.)

Activity 3   *Practice It!*

Summarize each item below by using the words in parentheses and *as . . . as*. Put the verb in the correct tense. Many sentences will be negative. You may include auxiliary verbs at the ends of your sentences, but they are never necessary. Study the examples carefully. Sometimes you must reverse the order of the ideas as in the second example below, or your sentences will be untrue.

Examples:

Larry is 38. Sarah is 38. (be / old)

Larry is as old as Sarah (is).

Barry explains things very, very clearly. Larry explains things pretty clearly.

Larry does not explain things as clearly as Barry (does).

1. Larry is about six feet tall. Smoch is about four feet tall. (be / tall)

2. Paula is 25 years old. Smoch is 3,583 years old. (be / old)

3. Paula got an A in English composition. Barry got an A in that class. (write / well)

4. The Altair 8800 is hard to program. The Apple II is easy to program. (be / easy to program)

5. By 1980, Jobs had $165 million. Woz had $88 million. (be / rich)

6. Sarah's engines run noisily. Larry's engines run almost silently. (run / quietly)

7. A strong person can ride a bicycle at about 35 miles an hour. A cheetah can run 70 miles an hour. (A strong person cannot ride / fast / cheetah / run)

8. A large kangaroo can jump 40 feet. A top human athlete can jump about 29 feet. (jump / far)

9. The adventure movie has a rating of three stars. The science fiction movie has a rating of three stars. (be / good)

10. This book is 8.25 inches wide. It is 10.88 inches long. (be / wide / it is long)

Larry's ship

Sarah's ship

❶ Use *as many . . . as* to indicate equal numbers of countable nouns.

> Sarah's ship does not have **as many** portholes **as** Larry's.
>
> (OR: Sarah's ship does not have the same number of portholes as Larry's.)

❷ Use *as much . . . as* to express equality with uncountable nouns and verbs.

> a. **Uncountable nouns:** Sarah does not have **as much** information about the aliens **as** Larry.
>
> (OR: Sarah does not have the same amount of information about the aliens as Larry.)
>
> b. **Verbs:** Nobody else knew **as much** about the design of the Apple II **as** Woz.

❸ You may find variations on this structure.

> a. Paula did not study **as hard** in high school **as** in college.
>
> (= She studied a little in high school. She studied hard in college.)
>
> b. There are **almost as many** aliens on Quarafanaflou **as** people in New York.
>
> (= There are 8,000,000 aliens on Quarafanaflou. There are about 9,000,000 people in New York.)

Activity 4   *Practice It!*

In each item, write a negative sentence using the word or words in parentheses and
as much . . . as or *as many . . . as.* You may include auxiliary verbs at the ends of your
sentences, but they are never necessary. (**Note:** Begin your sentence with the first word of the
sentence given, not with the word in parentheses.)

Examples:

The Altair 8800 could do things. (The Apple II)

The Altair 8800 could not do as many things as the Apple II (could).

There were not many personal computers in the world in 1976. (today).

There were not as many personal computers in the world in 1976 as there are today.

1. Sarah has friends. (Barry)
2. Smoch knows English. (Paula)
3. Computers in the 1950s could process information. (modern computers)
4. A four-person fishing boat uses fuel. (Larry's boat)
5. There are whales in the oceans. (insects in the forests)
6. Paula earns money. (Barry)

7. Motorcycles pollute the air. (cars)
8. A professional chess player receives letters from fans. (a movie star)
9. Adolescents need sleep. (newborn babies)
10. There are trees in the desert. (in the rain forest)

Activity 5   *Use It!*

Work with a partner that comes from a different country than you do. After talking about your
two countries, write at least five sentences with *as . . . as* or *not as . . . as* comparing your two
countries and their people. (**Note:** If you cannot find a partner from a different country, you
and your partner can write about two animals, two cars, two airplanes, or whatever you like.)

Examples:

Soccer is as popular in France as in Indonesia.

People in Indonesia don't eat as much cheese as people in France.

 **Lesson 3**

Comparatives and Superlatives of Superiority

Points to Remember: Short and Irregular Adjectives ·····················

❶ Here are some examples of the comparative form of short adjectives.

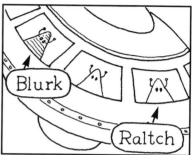

a. Blurk's skin is **darker than** Raltch's.

   (= Raltch's skin is not as dark as Blurk's.)

b. Modern computers are **faster than** early ones.

❷ Short adjectives include adjectives with one syllable and adjectives with two syllables that end in *-le, -er,* or *-ow.* Add *-er* to short adjectives to make the comparative.

a. small ➔ smaller
c. fast ➔ faster
e. clever ➔ cleverer

b. long ➔ longer
d. little ➔ littler
f. narrow ➔ narrower

❸ *Exceptions:* Add only *-r* to adjectives ending in *e*: brave ➔ braver

Change final *-y* to *i* and add *-er*: happy ➔ happier[1]

Double the final consonant of adjectives ending in one vowel and one consonant before adding *-er*: fat ➔ fatter[2]

The following short adjectives have irregular comparative forms:

a. good ➔ better
b. bad ➔ worse
c. far ➔ farther

Activity 6   Practice It!

Write the comparative forms of the following short adjectives.

Example:

big ➔ *bigger*

1. slow
2. fast
3. funny

4. far
5. nice
6. shallow

7. hot
8. good
9. little

10. clever
11. nasty
12. bad

---

[1] Do not change the -y if there is a vowel before it: gray ➔ grayer
[2] Do not double w, x, or y: slow ➔ slower, lax ➔ laxer, gray ➔ grayer

Write a sentence with the same meaning as the sentence given. You may need to make some adjustments in your new sentences. Extra help is given with some of the more difficult items like the second example. You may include auxiliary verbs at the ends of your sentences, but they are never necessary.

Examples:

The air on Earth is not as warm as the air on Quarafanaflou.

The air on Quarafanaflou is warmer than the air on Earth (is).

Smoch writes Chinese pretty well. He doesn't speak Greek well at all. (Smoch writes . . . he . . . Greek.)

Smoch writes Chinese better than he speaks Greek.

1. Sarah is not as nice as Paula.
2. Paula is not as tall as Barry.
3. Larry's handwriting is not as bad as Sarah's.
4. Jupiter is not as far from Earth as Quarafanaflou. (Quarafanaflou . . . from Earth . . . Jupiter.)
5. The Altair 8800 was not as cheap as the Apple II.
6. Paula is not as pretty as her sister. (Paula's . . .)

7. A highway is not as narrow as a path.
8. The weather in England is not as warm as the weather in Nigeria.
9. Canadian food is not as hot as Thai food.
10. Birds do not seem as bright as dolphins.

Point to Remember: Other Comparisons of Superiority • • • • • • • • • • • • • • • • • • •

All comparative forms other than those of short and irregular adjectives include the word *more*.

a. **Long adjective:**[1] Paula's job is **more dangerous than** Barry's.

b. **Adverb:**[2] Larry's ship moves **more quietly** through the water **than** Sarah's.

c. **Quantity:** There is **more oxygen** on Earth **than** on Quarafanaflou.

d. **Verb:** Sarah smokes **more than** she should.

---

[1] Long adjectives include all adjectives that are not irregular or short, as defined in Points 2 and 3 on page 38.

[2] The comparative of one-syllable adverbs like *fast* is formed with *-er*. Examples: *fast → faster, hard → harder, soon → sooner.* The comparative of *well* is *better.*

Activity 8   *Practice It!*

Write the comparative forms of the following adjectives.

Examples:

big   →   *bigger*
important   →   *more important*

1. expensive   4. beautiful   7. thick   10. brave
2. far   5. clever   8. powerful   11. complicated
3. dangerous   6. interesting   9. shallow   12. bad

Activity 9   *Practice It!*

Make comparative sentences using the structures presented above. Be sure your sentences are true. You may include auxiliary verbs at the ends of your sentences, but they are never necessary. Check all subject-verb agreement.

Examples:

Computers / versatile

Computers are more versatile than calculators (are).

People in Asia / eat / rice

People in Asia eat more rice than people in Canada. (do).

1. The aliens' spaceship / move / quickly
2. For Smoch / human languages / difficult
3. The Pacific Ocean / contain / water
4. For astronomers / telescopes / useful
5. Paula / speak to Sarah / carefully
6. Dolphins / swim / easily

7. Radio announcers / speak / rapidly
8. Doctors / earn / money
9. People / speak / Chinese
10. First-class travel / expensive

Activity 10   *Use It!*

Step 1: In this activity, you will try to convince your classmates to "buy" your product instead of your competitor's. Work with a partner. (**Note:** Your partner will actually be your competitor, and you will be working *against* him or her.) With your partner/competitor, choose one kind of product that you would both like to "sell" in competition with each other. Here are some possibilities:

pain medicines	speed boats	vacation packages
canned spaghetti sauces	CD players	make-up
roller blades	detergent	telephone service

Step 2: Find magazine advertisements for two different brands of the kind of product that you and your partner have agreed upon. You will "sell" one brand. Your partner/competitor will "sell" the other. Study your ad and that of your partner/competitor. *Without talking,* write down as many comparative sentences as you can about the advantages of your product and the disadvantages of your partner/competitor's product. Use as many different comparative structures as you can. Do not show your sentences to your partner/competitor.

Examples:

The Apple II is cheaper than the Altair 8800.

The Altair is not as easy to program as the Apple.

Step 3: With your partner/competitor, visit another pair of students that have chosen different kinds of products. They will be your "customers." Using the sentences from Step 2, try to "sell" your product to the "customers." The "customers" choose the product they prefer and write down their reasons using comparative structures. Finally, reverse roles. Your "customers" become "sellers" and try to convince you to buy their products.

Points to Remember: Superlatives of Superiority ·····························

❶ Here are examples of the superlative forms of short and irregular adjectives.

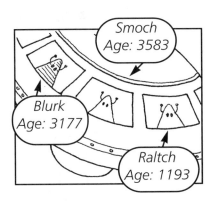

   a. Smoch is **the oldest** alien in the spaceship.
      (= The others are younger than he.)

   b. The Coast Guard gave Barry their **fastest** ship for Project Alien.

   c. Barry was **the best** student in his class.

❷ The superlative form follows the same spelling rules as the comparative form.

   a. small ➔ smaller ➔ **the smallest**

   b. brave ➔ braver ➔ **the bravest**

   c. happy ➔ happier ➔ **the happiest**

   d. fat ➔ fatter ➔ **the fattest**

❸ *Good, bad,* and *far* have irregular superlative forms.

    a. good ➔ better ➔ **the best**   c. bad ➔ worse ➔ **the worst**

    b. far ➔ farther ➔ **the farthest**

❹ The word *the* or a possessive almost always comes before the superlative form.

    a. Barry was **the** best student in his class.

    b. The Coast Guard gave Barry **their** fastest ship.

❺ Superlatives of long adjectives, adverbs, quantities, and verbs include the words *the* (or a possessive) and *most*.

    a. **Long adjective:** The IBM is one of **today's most popular** computers.

    b. **Adverb:** Project Alien is one of **the most carefully** guarded secrets of the U.S. government.

    c. **Quantity:** Of all mammals, young whales drink **the most** milk.

    d. **Verb:** Paula has swum with ducks, geese, and sea lions, but she **enjoys** swimming with dolphins **the most.**

Activity 11   *Practice It!*

Write a sentence with the same meaning as the sentence given. You may need to rearrange the sentences completely, as in the examples. Use the words in parentheses to help you.[1]

Examples:

No other character in the story is as nasty as Sarah. (Sarah is . . .)

Sarah is the nastiest character in the story.

No other private yacht is longer than the 282-foot yacht that was originally owned by Adnan Kashoggi. (The 282-foot yacht that . . . world.)

The 282-foot yacht that was originally owned by Adnan Kashoggi is the longest in the world.

1. No other computer is faster than the Cray Supercomputer. (The Cray . . . the world.)
2. No other navigator in the universe is as great as Smoch. (Smoch . . .)
3. No other person in Project Alien worries as much as Barry. (Barry . . . of all members of Project Alien.)
4. Sperm whales sometimes go down to a depth of more than 9,800 feet. No other marine mammal dives as deeply as the sperm whale. (The sperm whale . . . of all marine mammals.)
5. No other character in the story is as old as Smoch. (Smoch . . .)

---

[1] The source of the world records is the *Guiness Book of Records* (Bantam Books, 1992).

6. No carrot ever weighed more than the 15-pound 7-ounce carrot grown by I. Scott in New Zealand in 1978. (The 15-pound 7-ounce carrot grown . . .)

7. No other human language has more words than English. (Of all human languages, English . . .)

8. Five hundred years ago in China, no artist was as great as Wu Wei. (Five . . . Wu Wei . . . in China.)

9. Only a few works of art are as famous as the *Mona Lisa.* (The *Mona Lisa* . . . one of the . . . in the world.)

10. Derick Herning speaks 22 languages. Nobody speaks more languages than Mr. Herning. (Derick Herning . . . of anybody in the world.)

Activity 12 *Use It!*

Step 1: Play the "Superlative Quiz Game." Divide into teams of from three to five students. Choose a good name for your team. Without referring to any books, each team makes up as many questions as possible about world records. The team has to be sure of the answers. A team will lose points for asking a question if they don't know the answer.

Examples:

What's the longest river in the world?

Who is the highest paid musician of all time?

Step 2: The teams take turns asking their questions, one question in each turn. The other teams score a point for giving the correct answer first. At the end of the class, the team with the most points wins.

 **Lesson 4**

Comparatives and Superlatives of Inferiority

Points to Remember: Comparatives of Inferiority ··

❶ The comparative of inferiority is *fewer . . . than* for quantities of countable nouns.

Sarah has **fewer friends than** Barry.

(= Sarah's friends < Barry's friends)

❷ All other comparatives of inferiority include the words *less . . . than.*

    a. **Adjective:**   The Altair was **less popular than** the Apple II.

    b. **Adverb:**   Larry speaks **less angrily than** his cousin.

    c. **Uncountable quantity:**   In college, Sarah had **less difficulty** with political science **than** with English literature.

    d. **Verb:**   Humans **dream less than** the aliens.

Activity 13   *Practice It!*

Write a sentence with the same meaning as the sentence given. Use *less* or *fewer* in each sentence. In some items, you may include auxiliary verbs, but they are never necessary.

Examples:

A telescope does not cost as much as a ship.
A ship costs less than a telescope (does).

Not as many people live in Ottawa as in Toronto.
Fewer people live in Ottawa than in Toronto.

1. Larry thinks that art is not as interesting as science.
2. Dolphins are not in as much danger of extinction as gray whales.
3. Earth's sunsets are not as spectacular as Quarafanaflou's.
4. Paula did not learn long division as easily as Larry.
5. Many people believe that IBM computers are not as user-friendly as Apples.
6. Not as much money was spent on space research as on defense last year.
7. The wind does not blow as much in New York as in Chicago.
8. In the U.S., the Catholic Church is not growing as rapidly as the Protestant Churches.
9. Not as many symphonies were written by Beethoven as by Mozart.
10. Oranges do not contain as much protein as rice.

Points to Remember: Superlatives of Inferiority ···················

❶ The superlative of inferiority is *the fewest* for quantities of countable nouns.

> Of all the students in his class, Barry made **the fewest** mistakes on math exams. (= Nobody made fewer mistakes.)

❷ All other superlatives of inferiority include the words *the least*.

a.	**Adjective:**	Sarah is one of **the least friendly** people in the world.
b.	**Adverb:**	Of the three aliens, Smoch studied English **the least successfully.**
c.	**Uncountable quantity:**	Of all the courses she took at college, marine biology gave Paula **the least trouble.**
d.	**Verb:**	Paula has swum with many animals. She **enjoys** swimming with ducks **the least.**

Activity 14   *Practice It!*

Fill in each blank with *the least* or *the fewest* and the best word from the list below. Do not use any word twice.

cookies	fuel	✓ mistakes	likely
interesting	✓ uncomfortable	dangerous	expensive
well	fat	humid	protection
programs			

Examples:

No part of a 19th century whaling ship was pleasant to live in, but the captain's cabin was always _____ *the least uncomfortable* _____.

On a math test, the best paper is the one with _____ *the fewest mistakes* _____.

1. On Quarafanaflou, almost nobody buys Axamaka Space Cars because, of all major space car brands, Axamaka offers _____ from injury in space accidents.

2. Because of her unpleasant personality, Sarah would not make a very good political candidate. In fact, of all brilliant people in the United States, she is probably _____ person to be elected President.

3. Larry doesn't like to spend a lot of money on cars. His new car is _____ one he could find, and he says it is just what he wanted. One thing that he really likes about it is that, of all cars in its price range, it uses _____.

4. Most of the scientists on Larry's team have no interest in fashion. Nobody dresses well. Scientist Marla Garcia dresses _____. She usually wears mismatched patterns, and last Tuesday, she came to work with her sweater on inside-out!

5. Any time you travel on Earth you run the risk of accidents; however, mile for mile, modern airplanes are _____ way to go. Of course, the aliens' spaceship is much safer!

6. People that watch _____ on TV often read the most books.

7. Smith's Turkey Hot Dogs are the healthiest because they contain

   _____.

8. My friend and I went to a movie last night. It was probably _____ movie I've ever seen. I fell asleep after twenty minutes.

9. The thinnest people are usually the ones that eat _____ and other unhealthy snacks.

10. No rain falls in the Atacama Desert in Chile; in fact, it is _____ place on Earth.

Activity 15   *Use It!*

Step 1: There are too many people on Earth! You and your classmates will have to move to a distant planet, Bodo. Bodo's laws require immigrants to arrive in groups of three or four, and then to live together in the same city for five years. Groups have three cities to choose from: Dulia, Karb, and the capital, Slerx. In this activity, you and two or three classmates will choose the city where you will spend the next five years. First, working alone, rank the "City Characteristics" below from 1 to 8, in order of their importance to you. For example, if you think that a city's average salary is the most important, put a 1 in the blank next to "Salaries." If crime is the least important, rate "Crime" number 8. (**Note:** You must put a different number in each blank.)

The Planet Bodo

City Characteristics

___ Arts	___ Education
___ Basic costs of living	___ Recreation
___ Climate	___ Salaries
___ Crime	___ Transportation

Step 2: Working alone, study the information about the three Bodoan cities on the next page to decide where you prefer to live. Use the ranking that you made in Step 1 to help you. For example, if you ranked "Salaries" as number 1, look at salary information first.

General Description		Dulia	Karb	Slerx
	Population	20,000	500,000	7,000,000
	Location	In the mountains	Near the coast	On the plains in the middle of the continent.
	Economy	Electronics, dairy farms	Glass, auto manufacturing, fishing	Capital city, center of trade and industry
Arts and Entertainment				
	TV stations	1	3	7
	Concerts per year	10	170	616
	Museums	3	4	74
Basic Costs (B$/year)[1]				
	Food, clothing, housing, and taxes for a family of four	50,000	74,000	62,000
Climate				
	Sunny days per year	157	110	60
	Freezing days per year	3	13	92
	Days over 90 degrees F	4	7	61
	Rainfall	35″	43″	76″
Crimes per 100,000 people				
	Murders	0.8	3.3	8.2
	Robberies	19	29	64
Education				
	Adults with Bachelors Degree	29%	17%	34%
	Teachers with Masters Degree	45%	21%	61%
Recreation				
	Golf holes per 100,000 people	4	18	10
	Three–star restaurants per 100,000 people	0	2	8
	Other	wonderful area for hiking and camping	miles of beaches, wonderful water sports nearby	more bowling alleys per capita than any other city
Salaries (B$/year)				
	Engineer	60,000	90,000	110,000
	Mechanic	42,000	40,000	55,000
	Office worker	39,000	38,000	52,000
	Teacher	50,000	75,000	80,000
Transportation				
	Average daily commute	14 minutes	27 minutes	83 minutes
	Time to interplanetary port	38.5 hours	7.5 hours	0.5 hours

[1] B$ = Bodo dollars

Step 3: Work in "Traveling Groups" of three or four. All the members of your group must agree to live in the same Bodoan city for five years. If you do not agree with the other members of your group, try to convince the others that your choice is best. One person in your group is to give a report to the whole class on your group's decision. In the report, he or she could include sentences like:

Examples:

The majority of the students in our group chose to live in Karb.

For Bronislav, safety is the most important thing, so he wanted to live in Dulia because that city has the fewest crimes.

Even though Slerx has the most bowling alleys, and Ratana loves to bowl, she thinks she would have to spend too much time commuting in that city. Therefore, she prefers to live in Karb. The average commute is not as long in Karb as in Slerx.

Step 4: Working alone, write at least five sentences about the preferences of the members of your group. Use a different comparative or superlative structure in each sentence. Your sentences will be similar to the speaker's sentences in Step 3.

Chapter 6

ADVERB CLAUSES
AND SOME OTHER WAYS TO COMBINE IDEAS

Part 1

 Lesson 1

Adverb Clauses: The Basics

Points to Remember: Adverb Clauses ···

1 The clauses in dark letters in the sentences below are **adverb clauses**. Adverb clauses express relationships between ideas.

 a. Paula will be in danger **until she leaves Sarah's ship.**

 b. The scientists are excited **because this is their first contact with creatures from another planet.**

 c. Barry is **so** pleasant **that most people like him immediately.**

 d. Smoch is the navigator on the spaceship **even though he has already retired.**

 e. Paula is on Sarah's ship **so that she can trick the evil genius.**[1]

2 Every adverb clause is a weak clause. A weak clause is not a sentence in writing. When you write an adverb clause, you must write a strong clause with it. (**Note:** In speaking, this is not always necessary.)

 a. **Complete sentence:** Scientists are excited because this is their first contact with creatures from another planet.

 b. **Incomplete sentence:** Because this is their first contact with creatures from another planet.

---

[1] The connector *so that* in example e. is different from the connector *so . . . that* in example c. Example e. explains Paula's goal or purpose. The sentence means: "Paula is on Sarah's ship. Her goal is to trick Sarah." Example c. shows cause and effect. The sentence means: "Most people like Barry immediately because he is very pleasant."

3 Words such as *until, because,* and *so . . . that* are **connectors.**[1] They may be at the beginning of the sentence or in the middle. When the connector is in the beginning of the sentence, you must use a comma.

comma

Until Paula leaves Sarah's ship, she will be in serious danger.

4 When the connector is in the middle of the sentence, a comma is not usually used.

no comma

Paula will be in danger **until** she leaves Sarah's ship.

Activity 1   *Analyze It!*

Underline the adverb clause in each sentence once. Underline the connector twice. If a comma is necessary, add one.

Examples:

By the time Barry graduated from the Coast Guard Academy, he was one of the most popular students in his class.

The crops grew well even though it didn't rain much. (no comma)

1. Larry will try to communicate with the aliens after they land.
2. Since Paula first swam with a dolphin five years ago she has been very interested in marine mammals.
3. Larry's ship is equipped with a radio telescope because he needs to listen to the signals coming from the aliens' ship.
4. Until Paula is safe on land again Barry will be very nervous.
5. The aliens and the whales seem to have something in common even though they have never seen each other.

6. After he had played on the beach for three hours nonstop the little boy took a long nap.
7. The crowd stood up and cheered as soon as the referee declared the winner.
8. Because tofu contains a lot of protein many vegetarians eat it often.
9. Though television can certainly make our lives interesting it may be having a negative effect on the children.
10. None of the villagers believed the shepherd boy since he had tricked them several times before.

---

[1] The traditional name for connectors like *because* and *even though* is *subordinating conjunctions*.

Lesson 2

Time Clauses

Points to Remember ••

❶ Adverb **time clauses** begin with expressions such as *when, before,* and *as long as.*

a. *When* **Sarah heard about Larry's discovery,** she developed her evil plan.

b. *Before* **Paula went to college,** she had never used a computer.

c. *After* **Barry graduated,** he was given an important assignment.

d. *By the time* **Paula graduated from college,** she had spent hundreds of hours working on computers.   (*By the time* = *not after that time*)

e. *While*⎫ **Larry was talking,** everyone was very attentive.
   As ⎭

f. Barry and Paula have been in love *since* **they met.**

g. The Coast Guard will surround Sarah's ship *until* **Larry makes contact with the aliens.**

h. *As long as* **Sarah doesn't look at the computer screen,** she will have no way of knowing that Paula is giving her false information.
(*As long as* = *during the time that*)

i. Paula and Barry plan to get married *as soon as* **they can.**

❷ We do not use future tenses after time connectors.

a. **Correct:**   When Larry **reaches** the alien ship, he will try to communicate with the aliens.

b. **Incorrect:** When Larry will reach . . .

c. **Correct:**   The Coast Guard will surround Sarah's ship until Larry **makes** contact with the aliens.

d. **Incorrect:** . . . until Larry will make contact with the aliens.

Activity 2   *Practice It!*

Choose the best word or expression for each blank.

Example:

_____*As soon as*_____ Sarah heard about the aliens coming to Earth, she
  a. Until
✓ b. As soon as

_____*knew*_____ that she wanted to make a deal with them.
✓ a. knew
  b. knows

1. _____ Paula arrived on Sarah's ship, she _____ Sarah's
  a. Before   a. connected
  b. As soon as   b. connects

   computer to the Coast Guard network.

2. _____ Paula remains on Sarah's ship, Barry _____ able to relax.
  a. Until   a. has not been
  b. As long as   b. will not be

3. Barry entered the Coast Guard Academy at the age of eighteen. He remained a student
   there _____ he _____ at the age of twenty-two.
    a. until   a. will graduate
    b. as soon as b. graduated

4. Paula has been working hard _____ she _____ on the evil
                  a. since   a. arrives
                  b. until   b. arrived
   genius's ship.

5. Barry _____ worried about Paula's
        a. is
        b. will be

   safety _____ she gets off Sarah's ship.
        a. as long as
        b. until

(**Note:** This picture is right now.)

6. Fifteen-year-old Max has bought a used car, but he won't be able to drive it legally

   _____ he _____ sixteen. That's the law in his state.
  a. as long as   a. is
  b. until   b. will be

7. Sylvia and Ricardo went dancing the other night, and they closed the place down.

_____ they were ready to stop dancing, three of the band's eight
   a. While
   b. By the time

musicians _____ home.
   a. will already go
   b. had already gone

8. _____ the number of nationally known fast food restaurants increased,
   a. Until
   b. As

the number of small, privately owned restaurants _____.
   a. decreased
   b. will decrease

9. Ben is the new president of the International Student Association.

_____ he became the president, he _____ two meetings.
   a. Since   a. has already held
   b. Until   b. will already hold

10. _____ you put the noodles in the boiling water, you _____
   a. Until   a. let
   b. After   b. lets

them cook for about eight minutes, or _____ they are done.
   a. before
   b. until

Activity 3   *Use It!*

Choose one item from each pair below and write a complete sentence with an adverb time clause using the words given. Put five of the connectors at the beginning of the sentence and five in the middle. Pay attention to verb tenses and to punctuation.

Examples:

when / space   OR   when / see

When astronauts go into space, they become weightless.

before / morning   OR   before / evening

I lay looking at the ceiling for about twenty minutes before I got up this morning.

1. when / doctor   OR   when / wind
2. before / clothes   OR   before / vacation
3. after / TV   OR   after / visa
4. while / homework   OR   while / horse
5. as soon as / tomorrow OR   as soon as / yesterday
6. until / five years old OR   until / arrive
7. by the time / get up OR   by the time / police
8. since / arrive   OR   since / accident
9. as long as / refuse OR   as long as / money
10. as / eat   OR   as / test

 # Lesson 3

Reducing Time Clauses

Points to Remember ·

❶ A time clause beginning with *before, after,* or *since* can be reduced when it has the same subject as the main clause of the sentence. The *-ing* form is used.

a. **Correct:**   **Before entering** the Coast Guard Academy, Barry considered a career in business.

    Correct: Before he entered. . .

b. **Correct:**   **Since arriving** on Sarah's ship, Paula has been careful.

    Correct: Since she arrived. . .

c. **Correct:**   Larry will ask the aliens for a ride in their spaceship **after meeting** them.

    Correct: . . . after he meets them.

❷ Time clauses beginning with *while* and *as* can be reduced with *while* + verb + *-ing*, but not with *as* + verb + *-ing*.

a. **Correct:**   Sarah had dreams of great power **while developing** her plans.

b. **Correct:**   Sarah had dreams of great power $\begin{Bmatrix} \text{while} \\ \text{as} \end{Bmatrix}$ she developed her plans.

3 Time clauses beginning with *when* can be reduced in two different ways, depending on the meaning. Sometimes *when* means *every time*. In this case, the clause can be reduced with the word *when* + verb + *-ing*.

    a. **Correct:**   **When** working, Larry drinks tea.

    b. **Correct:**   **Every time** } he works, Larry drinks tea.
                        When

4 Other times, *when* means *as soon as*. In this case, the clause can be reduced with *upon* or *on*. (Clauses beginning with *as soon as* can be reduced in the same way.)

    a. **Correct:**   **Upon** } meeting, Barry and Paula fell in love.
                     On

    b. **Correct:**   **As soon as** } Barry and Paula met, they fell in love.
                       When

Activity 4   *Practice It!*

Reduce each time clause with *upon* (or *on*) or with *when*, depending on the meaning. Make any necessary changes in nouns and pronouns.

Examples:

When Larry listens to the aliens' signals, he tries to imagine their world.

When listening to the aliens' signals, Larry tries to imagine their world.

When Ms. Enriquez landed in New York, she called her office.

Upon (OR On) landing in New York, Ms. Enriquez called her office.

1. When Larry received the grant money, he hired six people to work with him.
2. When Sarah bought her ship, she went for a short cruise.
3. When Smoch returned to Quarafanaflou from the planet Yithrin, he declared that he would never travel in space again.
4. When Sarah rides in her ship, she sometimes feels a little seasick.
5. When he navigates the spaceship, Smoch goes into a deep trance.

6. When John cuts onions, he always holds a piece of bread between his teeth.
7. When Fred kicked the ball last night, he felt sure it would enter the goal.
8. When Julie received her first paycheck, she left for the mall.
9. When he entered the room, the president saw everybody stand up.
10. When Aladdin found the magic lamp, he rubbed it as hard as he could.

Points to Remember: More About Reducing Time Clauses · · · · · · · · · · · · · · · · · · ·

1 An adverb clause can be reduced only if it has the same subject as the main clause.

Sarah = she (same subject)

S ← → S

a. **Full form:**   While Sarah was developing her plan, she had dreams of great power.

b. **Reduced form:**   While developing her plan, Sarah had dreams of great power.

2 If the subjects of the two clauses are different, the time clause cannot be reduced. If it is reduced, the meaning is wrong.

Paula ≠ Larry (different subjects)

S ← → S

a. **Full form:**   While Paula swam with the dolphin, Larry gave a talk.

b. **Incorrect reduction:**   While swimming with the dolphin, Larry gave a talk.

(This sentence means that Larry gave a talk while he was swimming with a dolphin.)

3 The word *while* is often omitted when it comes at the beginning of a sentence.

a. **Correct:**   Listening to Larry's talk, Sarah made her evil plans.

b. **Correct:**   While listening to Larry's talk, Sarah made her evil plans.

4 Time clauses with *by the time, as long as,* and *until* cannot usually be reduced.

David Lang was a farmer in Tennessee. On September 23, 1900, he disappeared in the middle of his field—a field of short grass with no trees or rocks to hide a man! Reduce the adverb time clauses if possible.

Examples:

Before Mr. Lang disappeared, his wife gave him a glass of iced tea on the porch of their farm house.

The time clause cannot be reduced.

After he finished the iced tea, Mr. Lang stood up.

After finishing the iced tea, Mr. Lang stood up.

1. After Mr. Lang stood up, he walked down the steps from the porch.

2. As soon as he left the porch, he started walking across his field.

3. While he was walking across his field, his wife's brother and the local lawyer were driving their carriage to the Lang home for a visit.

4. When Lang reached the middle of the field, he disappeared.

5. As soon as Lang disappeared, the two visitors ran to look for him in the field.

6. By the time the two visitors reached the middle of the field, there was no sign of Lang.

7. When the two visitors studied the area, they could find nothing to help them understand the mystery of Lang's disappearance.

8. They searched until they were too tired to continue.

9. Ten months after Lang disappeared, the grass in a 20-foot circle in the middle of the field turned brown.

10. When animals approached the circle of dead grass, they would not touch it.

11. Since Lang disappeared, there have been many reports of UFO landings.

12. After UFOs leave the Earth, according to witnesses, there are often large areas of burnt grass; furthermore, animals always refuse to go near these areas.

13. Since they began to study the case of David Lang, some UFO experts have wondered if Lang was abducted by aliens.

14. Mrs. Lang never knew what had happened to her husband as long as she lived.

15. She received no information to help her understand the mystery before she died.

Activity 6   *Use It!*

Student 1 asks a question and chooses another student to answer it. Student 2 answers the question. The answer includes a reduced time clause.

Example:

What did you do after you left this class yesterday?

Student 1: *What did you do after you left this class yesterday?*

Student 2: *After leaving this class yesterday, I studied in the lounge.*

1. What did you do after you left this class yesterday?
2. How did you move around before you learned to walk?
3. What have you done since you got up today?
4. What do you usually do before you take a test?
5. Whom did you see when you entered the class today?
6. What do you usually think about while you walk from place to place?
7. When you were little, what did you usually do before you went to bed?
8. How have you changed since you left high school? (OR *middle school*)
9. What do you do after you get out of a swimming pool?
10. What was the first thing you did after you sat down in that chair?

Activity 7   *Use It!*

Think of any interesting person, for example, a movie director, the manager of a luxury hotel, or the leader of your country. Imagine what that person did last Wednesday. Then write sentences about that person's day using the structures below. Make your sentences interesting. Below, you can see an example of a good, interesting sentence. For contrast, there is also an example of an unimaginative, boring sentence.

Examples about a zoo keeper:

Good sentence: *As soon as Ms. Song arrived at the zoo, she prepared some special food for the African hedgehogs.*

Poor sentence: *As soon as Ms. Song got up, she washed her face.*

1. *when* (with a complete clause)
2. *before* (with a complete clause)
3. *by the time*
4. *as soon as*
5. *until*
6. *after* + verb + *-ing*
7. *while* + verb + *-ing*
8. *on* OR *upon* + verb + *-ing*

 **Lesson 4**

Clauses and Phrases Indicating Cause

Points to Remember: Cause Clauses •

❶ Adverb clauses beginning with certain words indicate cause.

    a. The world's scientists are excited *because* **the aliens are coming.**

    b. *Since* **Barry's fiancée is on Sarah's ship,** he is very nervous.

    c. Humans would die quickly on the aliens' planet *due to the fact that* **there is no oxygen there.**

    d. *Now that* **Larry can see the alien ship,** he is very excited.

    e. Larry and Sarah do not know each other well *as* **they have not spoken for years**.

❷ *Now that* indicates that something in the present situation is different from the past situation; something has changed. Only present focus verb tenses[1] should be used after *now that.*

    a. Barry is very happy now that he **has met** the girl of his dreams.
        (He had not met her before; his life has changed.)

    b. Barry is happy now that he **is going to get married.**
        (He was not planning to get married before.)

Activity 8   *Practice It!*

Without changing the order of the two clauses, combine them into one sentence using the connector given. You may need to make some other changes as in the second example below. Use commas when necessary.

    Examples:

    Barry was given an important job. Barry was the best student in his class. (because)
    Barry was given an important job because he was the best student in his class.

    The Smiths ran out of money. The Smiths returned from their vacation two days early. (since)
    Since the Smiths ran out of money, they returned from their vacation two days early.

---

[1] Present focus verb tenses are the simple present, present progressive, present perfect, present perfect progressive, and the after-present (or future) with *going to.*

1. Paula is giving Sarah false information. Sarah is heading in the wrong direction. (because)

2. Barry and Paula have many interests in common. Barry and Paula should have a happy marriage. (because)

3. Paula was upset with her roommate. Paula's roommate was very messy. (because)

4. Paula's picture is on Barry's wall. Paula is Barry's girl friend. (now that)

5. Humans do not know how to travel at speeds faster than the speed of light. It would take people years to reach the aliens' planet. (due to the fact that)

6. Mr. Kang has a black belt in karate. Most bullies leave Mr. Kang alone. (since)

7. The pilot became ill. One of the passengers had to fly the plane. (since)

8. Experts are very concerned about Africa's ability to feed itself in the future. Africa's population is increasing faster than that of any other continent. (due to the fact that)

9. The customers were unable to make any purchases. The store's computer was down. (due to the fact that)

10. The store's computer is running again. The customers are able to make their purchases. (now that)

Points to Remember: Prepositional Expressions of Cause · · · · · · · · · · · · · · · · · ·

❶ Several prepositional expressions can be used to indicate cause.

   a. Many people would refuse to do Paula's job **because of** the danger.

   b. In school, the other students avoided Sarah **on account of** her nasty personality.

   c. Barry succeeded in the Coast Guard Academy **owing to** his hard work.

   d. Larry's ability to move quickly is **due to** his boat's powerful engines.

   e. The aliens have been traveling faster than ever **thanks to** Smoch's navigational abilities.

❷ Because these are prepositional expressions, they can be followed by noun phrases. The connector *because*, on the other hand, must be followed by a clause.

                                              noun phrase

Many people would refuse to do Paula's job { **because of** the danger.
                                            { **because** it is so dangerous.
                                                  ————— **clause** —————

❸ These prepositional expressions cannot usually be followed by gerunds (the *-ing* form).

    a. **Correct:**   Barry succeeded owing to his hard work.

    b. **Incorrect:** Barry succeeded owing to working hard.

Activity 9   *Practice It!*

Reduce each adverb clause to a prepositional phrase using the expression given. Extra help is given in some of the more difficult items, like the second example below. Put one letter in each blank.

Examples:

Barry can see people on Sarah's ship because his binoculars are so strong. (because of)

Barry can see people on Sarah's ship because of his strong binoculars.

The president was unable to continue his work because he was ill.
(due to h _ _   i _ _ _ _ _ s)

The president was unable to continue his work due to his illness.

1. Paula got involved in Project Alien because she was interested in dolphins and whales.
   (because of h _ _   i _ _ _ _ _ _ _ _   i _ dolphins and whales)

2. Now that the computer network is so extensive, the Coast Guard is able to send information instantly around the world.
   (owing to i _ s   e _ _ _ _ _ _ _ _   c _ _ _ _ _ _ _   n _ _ _ _ _ _)

3. Smoch was chosen as navigator for the trip to Earth because he has wonderful mathematical abilities. (because of)

4. It is possible for Larry to move quickly because the sea is very calm. (because of)

5. People like Paula immediately because she has a nice smile. (on account of)

6. The field trip was canceled because it was raining heavily.
   (on account of h _ _ _ _   r _ _ _)

7. The corn grew poorly because there was very little rain.
   (because of a l _ _ _   o _   r _ _ _)

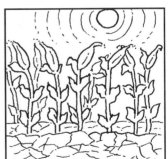

8. We gave the waiter a 20% tip because the service was superior. (because of)

9. There's a great deal of pollution in that city because the cars are poorly maintained. (on account of the p _ _ _ _ _ m _ _ _ _ _ _ _ _ _ cars)

10. The children stayed warm in the snow storm because they were wearing very warm clothes. (thanks to)

11. The drivers had to stop because it was very foggy. (due to)

12. The kids' day off was because it had snowed heavily the night before. (due to)

13. Now that Mr. Smith has a lot of money, all his relatives want to visit him. (because of)

14. Sandra was put on probation because her grades were poor. (because of)

15. Children were forbidden to see the movie because it contained many violent scenes. (because of it _ m _ _ _ v _ _ _ _ _ _ s _ _ _ _ s)

Activity 10   *Practice It!*

Read each strong clause first. Then guess which adverb phrase or clause might go with it. Match the adverb clauses with the adverb phrases that have similar meaning. Fill in each blank with one letter. Finally, write out each sentence two times: first with an adverb clause, and second with an adverb phrase. The two sentences will have similar meaning.

Strong clauses	Adverb clauses	Adverb phrases
1. Larry was able to continue his research	a. because it h a s many natural w o n d e r s.	c. b e c a u s e of i t s many n a t u r a l wonders.
2. Arizona is a popular vacation destination	b. b e c a u s e he r e c e i v e d money f r o m the government.	d. t h a n k s to money from t h e government.

Examples:

1. Larry was able to continue his research because he received money from the government.

Larry was able to continue his research thanks to money from the government.

2. Arizona is a popular vacation destination because it has many natural wonders.

Arizona is a popular vacation destination because of its many natural wonders.

Group 1

Strong clauses	Adverb clauses	Adverb phrases
1. The company is succeeding	a. n _ _ t _ _ _ it i _ making popular p _ _ _ _ _ _ s.	d. o _ _ _ g to its b _ _ _ _ _ _ _ _ rings.
2. Saturn is the most spectacular planet	b. because they _ _ _ so f _ _ _.	e. because o _ their sp _ _ d.
3. Many people like microwave ovens	c. b _ _ _ _ _ _ it has beautiful r _ _ _ _.	f. b _ _ _ _ s _ o _ the popular _ t _ of i _ _ products.

Group 2

Strong clauses	Adverb clauses	Adverb phrases
4. They had a nice time at the party	a. b _ _ _ _ _ _ t _ _ _ are very l _ _ _l.	d. due to her g _ _ _ e _ _.
5. Dogs are favorite pets	b. due t _ the fact t _ _ _ she has a good eye.	e. on a _ _ _ _ _ _ of e _ _ _ _o _ _ ' _ friendliness.
6. Her success in photography is	c. because everyone w _ _ so f _ _ _ _ d _ _.	f. o _ _ _ _ to their loyalty.

Group 3

Strong clauses	Adverb clauses	Adverb phrases
7. Sam lost points on his test	a. s _ _ _ _ the president h _ _ an important a _ _ _ _ n _ _ m _ _ _ to make.	e. on a _ _ _ _ _ _ of his c _ r _ lessn _ _ _.
8. The regularly scheduled program is canceled	b. because sh _ eats g _ _ _ f _ _ d.	f. d _ _ to an i _ _ _ _ t _ _ _ announcement from the president.
9. Paula is able to type quickly	c. b _ _ _ _ _ _ he was careless.	g. on a _ _ _ _ _ _ of her excellent d _ _ t.
10. Paula is in good health	d. n _ _ that she has t _ k _ _ typing l _ _ _ _ n _.	h. t _ _ _ _ _ to her t _ _ _ _ _ lessons.

Activity 11   *Use It!*

Interview another student in the class about the members of his or her family. Ask about family, jobs, hobbies, health, etc. Write eight sentences about those people: three sentences with *because* in the middle, three completely different sentences with *because* in the beginning, and two sentences with *because of*. (**Note:** Keep your sentences. You will need them for an activity in the next chapter.)

Examples:

(**Note:** Blurk, one of the aliens, took English classes before leaving for Earth. The examples are sentences another student wrote about members of Blurk's family.)

a sentence with *because* in the middle

Blurk's sister was called "Vegetable Woman" because she ate a lot of vegetables.

a sentence with *because* in the beginning

Because he saved the king's life, Blurk's grandfather was given a house in the mountains.

a sentence with *because of*

Blurk's grandfather was well known because of his bravery.

Chapter 7

ADVERB CLAUSES
AND SOME OTHER WAYS TO COMBINE IDEAS
Part 2

 Lesson 1

Reducing Cause Clauses to -ing Phrases

Points to Remember: Cause and Effect Over the Same Time ·················

❶ Cause clauses can sometimes be reduced to *–ing* phrases.[1] They almost always come at the beginning of a sentence.

   a. **Seeing nothing on the horizon,** Sarah is beginning to get upset.

     (= Because she sees nothing on the horizon, Sarah is beginning to get upset.)

   b. **Not wanting her plan to fail,** Sarah will do anything necessary to reach the aliens before Larry.

     (= Because she doesn't want her plan to fail, Sarah will do anything necessary to reach the aliens before Larry.)

❷ This type of reduction is most common when a cause and its effect continue over the same period of time.

   a. Seeing nothing on the horizon (now), Sarah is beginning to get upset (now).

   b. Being from a poor family (during his years at the Academy), Barry worked hard to get scholarships during his years at the Academy.

❸ This type of reduction is most common with three groups of verbs. The first group is verbs of condition like *be, consist, contain, cost, feel, have, look, measure, smell, sound, taste,* and *weigh.*

     Containing no oxygen at all, the air on the aliens' planet cannot support human life.

---

[1] *-Ing* phrases are traditionally called *participial phrases.*

④ The second group is verbs of mental activity like *believe, imagine, know, need, remember,* and *want*.

> **Imagining life on other worlds,** Larry is eager to travel in space.

⑤ The third group is verbs of the five senses like *feel, hear, see, smell,* and *taste*.

> **Smelling the salt in the air,** Larry is happy to be at sea.

Activity 1   *Practice It!*

Combine the two sentences into one beginning with an *-ing* phrase. You may need to change the order of the ideas or make changes in the nouns and pronouns.

Example:

Sarah called her banker to ask for a loan. Sarah needed a ship.

Needing a ship, Sarah called her banker to ask for a loan.

1. Smoch is the best navigator on his planet because he knows how to control a spaceship with his thoughts.
2. Radio telescopes are not bought by many people. They are expensive.
3. Barry is in love with Paula. Barry has Paula's picture on his wall.
4. The U.S. President has a special airplane. He can travel wherever and whenever he wants.
5. Ellie did not know about the quiz. She didn't study.

Point to Remember: Cause Before the Effect ·····································

The cause is often before the effect in time. In this case, the cause phrase begins with *having* + past participle. This structure can be used with all verbs.

a. **Having found** the alien ship on the horizon, Larry is heading west.

> (= He is heading west *now* because he found the ship *a few minutes ago.*)

b. **Having discovered** signals from outer space, Larry wrote a report.

> (= He wrote a report in April because he had discovered signals from outer space *a month before.*)

Activity 2   *Practice It!*

Combine the two sentences into one using *having* + a past participle. You may need to change the order of the ideas or make changes in nouns and pronouns.

Example:

Barry was given an important assignment. He had graduated at the top of his class.

Having graduated at the top of his class, Barry was given an important assignment.

1. The dolphin enjoyed playing with Paula the first time. He was looking forward to seeing her again.

2. Paula's roommate was too embarrassed to talk with her instructor. She had caused an explosion in the chemistry lab.

3. Raltch had learned seventeen human languages. He felt ready to come to Earth.

4. The workers will be hungry tomorrow night. The workers will not have eaten all day long.

5. Andrea repaired her car herself. She felt very proud.

Activity 3   *Practice It!*

In each item, decide which sentence is the cause and which is the effect. Then decide whether the cause is at the same time as the effect or before it. Finally, combine the two sentences with the correct type of *-ing* phrase.

Examples:

Larry wrote a report. He discovered intelligent signals from outer space.

The cause is   a. ☐ the first sentence.   b. ☑ the second sentence.
The cause is   a. ☐ at the same time as the effect.   b. ☑ before the effect.

Having discovered intelligent signals from outer space, Larry wrote a report.

The Red Team was stronger than the Blue Team. The Red Team defeated the Blue Team easily.

The cause is   a. ☑ the first sentence.   b. ☐ the second sentence.
The cause is   a. ☑ at the same time as the effect.   b. ☐ before the effect.

Being stronger than the Blue Team, the Red Team beat the Blue Team easily.

1. Paula volunteered for a dangerous job. She wanted to protect the world's animals.

   The cause is   a. ☐ the first sentence.   b. ☐ the second sentence.
   The cause is   a. ☐ at the same time as the effect.   b. ☐ before the effect.

2. Larry will be tired tonight. He will have worked hard all day long.

   The cause is   a. ☐ the first sentence.   b. ☐ the second sentence.
   The cause is   a. ☐ at the same time as the effect.   b. ☐ before the effect.

3. Paula was the best person for the job on Sarah's ship. She had received excellent computer training.

   The cause is   a. ☐ the first sentence.   b. ☐ the second sentence.
   The cause is   a. ☐ at the same time as the effect.   b. ☐ before the effect.

4. Paula was the best person for the job on Sarah's ship. She had excellent computer skills.

   The cause is   a. ☐ the first sentence.   b. ☐ the second sentence.
   The cause is   a. ☐ at the same time as the effect.   b. ☐ before the effect.

5. Blurk felt sad about leaving his planet. Blurk went to the local temple to communicate with his ancestors.

   The cause is   a. ☐ the first sentence.   b. ☐ the second sentence.
   The cause is   a. ☐ at the same time as the effect.   b. ☐ before the effect.

6. Larry needed money to continue his research. He applied for a grant.

   The cause is   a. ☐ the first sentence.   b. ☐ the second sentence.
   The cause is   a. ☐ at the same time as the effect.   b. ☐ before the effect.

7. Sandra wanted to talk with Phyllis. Sandra picked up the phone.

   The cause is   a. ☐ the first sentence.   b. ☐ the second sentence.
   The cause is   a. ☐ at the same time as the effect.   b. ☐ before the effect.

8. Regina had never learned to cook. She was looking for a roommate who was comfortable in the kitchen.

   The cause is   a. ☐ the first sentence.   b. ☐ the second sentence.
   The cause is   a. ☐ at the same time as the effect.   b. ☐ before the effect.

9. Sam didn't have any curtains. Sam covered his windows with newspaper.

   The cause is   a. ☐ the first sentence.   b. ☐ the second sentence.
   The cause is   a. ☐ at the same time as the effect.   b. ☐ before the effect.

10. The baseball player hit the ball out of the park. The baseball player ran around the bases.

The cause is   a. ☐ the first sentence.   b. ☐ the second sentence.

The cause is   a. ☐ at the same time as the effect.   b. ☐ before the effect.

Activity 4   *Use It!*

In Activity 11 on page 64, you wrote eight sentences about members of a classmate's family. Now, reduce the cause clauses if possible. Reduce the cause clause of all sentences in which the cause is before the effect. If the cause is at the same time as the effect, reduce the cause clause only if its verb is in one of the three groups listed in Points 3, 4, and 5 on pages 65 and 66 (or perhaps another verb with similar meaning).

Examples:

Blurk's sister was called "Vegetable Woman" because she ate a lot of vegetables.
(This cannot be reduced.)

Because he saved the king's life, Blurk's grandfather was given a house in the mountains.
→ Having saved the king's life, Blurk's grandfather was given a house in the mountains.

 **Lesson 2**

Effect Clauses

Points to Remember: The Connector *So . . . That* ·······························

❶ In the following examples, the first clause is the cause clause. The second clause is the effect clause. An adjective, adjective phrase, adverb, or adverb phrase comes between the words *so* and *that*.

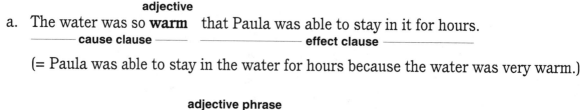

a. The water was so **warm** that Paula was able to stay in it for hours.
   ————— cause clause ————— ————————— effect clause —————————

   (= Paula was able to stay in the water for hours because the water was very warm.)

adjective phrase
b. The aliens' planet is so **far from Earth** that it would take many years for humans to travel there.

adverb
c. Larry explained his discovery so **clearly** that even the non-scientists in the crowd could understand.

——— **adverb phrase** ———
d. Dolphins move so **quickly through the water** that many boats can't keep up with them.

❷ The words *many* and *much* can also come between *so* and *that*. *Many* is used with plural countable nouns. *Much* is used with uncountable nouns.

plural noun
a. So **many people** attended Larry's talk that some of them had to stand up.

   (= A lot of people attended Larry's talk. As a result, some of them had to stand up.)

uncountable noun
b. Sarah had so **much money** that she was able to buy a ship.

Activity 5   *Practice It!*

Write a sentence with similar meaning to the sentence or sentences given. Use *so . . . that, so much . . . that,* or *so many . . . that* in each answer. Begin each sentence with the cause clause. You may need to reverse the order of the ideas and make changes in the nouns and pronouns as in the first example below. Do not use the word *because.*

Examples:

Barry can see people on Sarah's ship because his binoculars are very powerful.

Barry's binoculars are so powerful that he can see people on Sarah's ship.

The teacher has many students. She cannot remember all their names.

The teacher has so many students that she cannot remember all their names.

1. The water was shallow; as a result, Paula could easily stand up.

2. A great number of Coast Guard ships will surround Sarah; therefore, she will be unable to get to the aliens.

3. Whales are very big; consequently, the aliens will not be able to take one home in their spaceship.

4. A human would die immediately on the aliens' planet, for the air there is very poisonous.

5. You can't count the stars, for there is an unbelievably large number of them.

6. I cannot understand that woman because she speaks very quickly.

7. Ellen made no mistakes on her math test. She worked very carefully.

8. I could not see Peter because he had a great number of books on the table in front of him.

9. The media[1] bombard us with great quantities of information. We cannot digest all the information.

10. The restaurant gave me a great deal of food, so I took half of it home in a doggy bag.

Vocabulary

[1] media: the irregular plural of *medium*. Radio, newspapers, and TV are media.

Points to Remember: The Connector *Such . . . That* ·····················

❶ *Such . . . that* can also be used to express effect. A noun or noun phrase comes between *such* and *that*.

Examples with uncountable nouns:

noun
a. In his human language classes, Smoch had such **difficulty** that he finally gave up trying.

noun phrase
b. Barry did such **good work** that he graduated first in his class from the Coast Guard Academy.

Example with a plural countable noun:

—— noun phrase ——
c. Are the aliens such **strange creatures** that people will be afraid of them?

❷ When a singular countable noun follows *such*, the "small word"[1] *a* or *an* is necessary.

A blue whale is such **a** big animal that six of the aliens' spaceships could easily fit inside one of them.

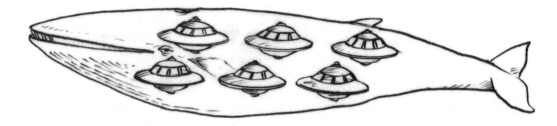

Activity 6   *Practice It!*

Choose the best word for each blank. Then combine the two sentences in each item into one with *such . . . that*. Do not change the order of the ideas.

challenging	✓ dangerous	nervous	cold	mysterious	soft
skilled	playful	expensive	✓ wonderful	nasty	entertaining

Examples:

Paula has a/an _____*dangerous*_____ job. Barry is worried about her.

They had _____*wonderful*_____ weather. They were able to go swimming every day.

Paula has such a dangerous job that Barry is worried about her.

They had such wonderful weather that they were able to go swimming every day.

---
[1] See page 11 for the presentation of "small words."

1. The dolphin was a/an _____ animal. Paula didn't want to get out of the ocean.

2. Sarah was a/an _____ child. All her classmates were afraid of her.

3. Sarah is a/an _____ person. She is often unable to sleep more than two or three hours a night.

4. The ocean is a/an _____ place. Scientists are just beginning to uncover its secrets.

5. Smoch is a/an _____ navigator. The elders asked him to come out of retirement to pilot the spaceship to Earth.

6. It's a very _____ book. You won't want to put it down.

7. It was _____ weather. Everybody wore gloves, boots, and hats.

8. The instructor gave a/an _____ test. Few in the class got "A."

9. It's a very _____ neighborhood. Only wealthy people can live there.

10. The kitten has _____ fur. All the children want to pet it.

Activity 7   *Practice It!*

Put *so, so much, so many, such, such an,* or *such a* in each blank.

Examples:

Sarah is _____ *so* _____ smart that she never had to study for tests at school.

The candidate gave _____ *such a* _____ good speech that the crowd stood up and cheered for seven minutes.

1. Paula had _____ fun with the dolphin that she returned again and again.

2. The computer system is _____ complicated that no one person can understand all the programming.

3. There are _____ planets in the sky that there must be life on some of them.

4. Barry has _____ friends from all over North America that he rarely has to stay in hotels when he travels.

5. Blurk is _____ interesting creature that Earth scientists will want to study him for years.

6. I ate _____ pizza that I had no room for dessert.

7. The restaurant has _____ good food that it's necessary to make reservations weeks in advance.

8. Sam's story was _____ strange that no one knew what to say.

9. It was _____ strange story that everyone was speechless.

10. The Titanic sank in _____ deep water that people couldn't reach it for many decades.

Activity 8   *Practice It!*

In each group, match each cause sentence on the left with the best effect sentence on the right. Then combine the two using *so . . . that, so much . . . that, so many . . . that,* or *such . . . that.*

Examples:

Causes

1. Paula has a dangerous job.

2. The student has many books.

Effects

a. She can't carry them all.

b. Barry is always worried about her.

1. Paula has such a dangerous job that Barry is always worried about her.

2. The student has so many books that she can't carry them all.

Group 1

Causes

1. The office is well organized.
2. Peter's a good waiter.
3. Many scientists wanted to go with Larry to meet the aliens.

Effects

a. It was necessary to have a lottery to choose a small number of them.

b. He often gets $100 in tips a night.

c. Everything gets done very quickly.

Group 2

Causes

4. Some baseball players make a lot of money.
5. Atoms are tiny.
6. Wolves are rare animals.

Effects

a. Billions of them can fit on the period at the end of this sentence.

b. They are hardly ever seen in North America.

c. They can't spend it all.

Group 3

Causes

7. Arnold is an honest person.

8. That magician knows a lot of tricks.

9. The movie was boring.

10. The aliens' spaceship is fast.

Effects

a. He tells the truth even when it hurts.

b. Many in the audience fell asleep.

c. It made the trip to Earth in only a few months.

d. He can perform for two hours without repeating any of them.

Activity 9   *Use It!*

Work in pairs. Draw three different sketches that illustrate a cause and an effect. Write as many sentences with different structures as you can for each picture.

Examples:

1. *The man is so tall that he cannot live in the house.*

2. *He is such a tall man that he cannot live in the house.*

3. *He is very tall, so he cannot live in the house.*

etc.

 **Lesson 3**

Concession Clauses

Activity 10   *Read It!*

Step 1: This conversation took place last Sunday. As you read it, pay attention to the adverb clauses in **dark** letters.

> **Barry:** Paula, I'm worried. I don't want you to go to Sarah's ship.
>
> **Paula:** Don't worry, darling! Your planning is excellent.
>
> **Barry:** **Even though my planning is excellent,** Sarah is extremely dangerous.
>
> **Paula:** My training has been complete. I'm the best person for the job. Nothing can go wrong.
>
> **Barry:** **Despite the fact that you're the best person for the job,** lots can go wrong. And no one on Sarah's ship will help you.

Step 2: Write *T* in the blank if the statement is true or *F* if it is false.

Examples:

  T   Barry is worried about Paula.

  F   Paula says that she is worried about her job on Sarah's ship.

  _____   1. Barry agrees with everything Paula says.

  _____   2. Barry agrees with parts of what Paula says.

  _____   3. Barry agrees with Paula that his planning is excellent.

  _____   4. Barry thinks that Paula is the best person for the job.

  _____   5. Barry agrees with Paula that nothing can go wrong on Sarah's ship.

Points to Remember: Concession Clauses ·····························

❶ In the conversation in Activity 10, Barry makes two **concessions** to Paula's arguments. In other words, he agrees that **parts** of her ideas are true. Then he makes his main points.

    ———— concession ———— ———— main point ————

a. Even though my planning is excellent, Sarah is extremely dangerous.

(= It is true that my planning for Project Alien is excellent, but Sarah is extremely dangerous.)

    ———— concession ———— ———— main point ————

b. Despite the fact that you're the best person for the job, lots can go wrong.

2 The five connectors[1] in **dark** letters below all have similar meaning. They are all commonly used at the beginning of a sentence. They are listed in approximate order of strength, from the weakest to the strongest.

Though
Although
Even though   } the plan is good, lots can go wrong.
In spite of the fact that
Despite the fact that

3 The three connectors in the example below are also commonly used in the middle of sentences. (**Note:** Students can avoid mistakes by not using *though* and *although* in the middle of sentences.)

Scientists know almost nothing about the aliens { **even though** **despite the fact that** **in spite of the fact that** } they

have been listening to the aliens' "songs" for years.

Activity 11   *Practice It!*

Choose ten of the items below and complete each sentence in a meaningful way. Then rewrite it with the connector in the beginning of the sentence. You may need to make some changes in nouns and pronouns. Punctuate your sentences correctly. You will need to use your imagination.

Example:

Larry wants to travel with the aliens even though . . .

Larry wants to travel with the aliens even though he doesn't know much about them.

Even though Larry doesn't know much about the aliens, he wants to travel with them.

1. Larry has no weapons on his ship even though . . .
2. Paula dreams of making a movie even though . . .
3. Paula swims in the ocean in February even though . . .
4. The aliens' songs are similar to whale songs in spite of the fact that . . .
5. The aliens' trip took only a few months despite the fact that . . .
6. Barry is worried about Paula even though . . .

---

[1] A sixth connector, *while*, can also be used with similar meaning. This word is sometimes confusing because it also has a time meaning: "While Larry was giving his speech, Paula was swimming with a dolphin."

7. Many people smoke cigarettes even though . . .

8. I entered the house even though . . .

9. Some people drive at 80 miles per hour in spite of the fact that . . .

10. Canadians bought more cars last month despite the fact that . . .

11. The Red Team beat the Blue Team even though . . .

12. The student was using a calculator during the test despite the fact that . . .

Points to Remember: Other Ways to Express Concession

❶ Concession clauses can be reduced to prepositional phrases with *in spite of* and *despite*. These words have the same meaning.

a. In February, Paula goes swimming $\begin{Bmatrix} \textbf{in spite of} \\ \textbf{despite} \end{Bmatrix}$ the cold water.

(= She goes swimming even though the water is cold.)

b. Larry read his paper $\begin{Bmatrix} \textbf{in spite of} \\ \textbf{despite} \end{Bmatrix}$ his nervousness.

(= He read his paper even though he was nervous.)

❷ Because *despite* and *in spite of* are prepositional expressions, they are followed by nouns or noun phrases. They are not usually followed by gerunds (verb + *-ing*).

Activity 12 *Practice It!*

Rewrite each sentence by changing the adverb clause to a prepositional phrase with *in spite of* or *despite*. The nouns you will need are listed below. You may need to add some other words or make some other small changes as in the second example.

diet	innocence	convenience	size	weight	✓ danger
✓ health	fear	speed	distance	inability	spiciness

Examples:

Paula accepted the assignment on Sarah's ship even though it was dangerous.

Paula accepted the assignment on Sarah's ship in spite of the danger.

In spite of the fact that he was sick, Barry played basketball with his friends.

Despite his poor health, Barry played basketball with his friends.

1. Raltch decided to go to Earth even though it was very far.

2. Blue whales can swim fast even though they weigh up to 150 tons.

3. Fin whales are often killed by hunters even though they are very fast.

4. The three aliens are comfortable in their spaceship even though it's small.

5. Although he is terrified of dentists, Barry went for a dental check-up.

6. Amish people refuse to drive cars even though they are very convenient.

7. The man was kept in jail despite the fact that he had committed no crimes.

8. Stephanie doesn't seem to be able to lose weight in spite of the fact that she is on a strict weight-loss program.

9. Though they can't fly, ostriches are birds.

10. I love Thai food even even though it's spicy hot.

Activity 13 *Use It!*

Paula has swum with dolphins dozens of times, but she doesn't really feel that she understands them. She wishes that she could **be** a dolphin, even for just an hour or two. In that way, she could truly understand these playful animals. If Paula could be a dolphin, she would have one problem, however. She doesn't like fish, and that is what dolphins eat. Therefore, Paula says, "Even though I don't like fish, I'd like to be a dolphin for a short time." In this activity, each student in the class should write a sentence about his or her favorite animal. The sentence should be similar to Paula's. Each student should say his or her sentence, and the others should try to remember it, in the style of the game "I Pack My Trunk."

Examples:

Paula: *Even though I don't like fish, I'd like to be a dolphin for a short time.*

Brian: *Even though Paula doesn't like fish, she'd like to be a dolphin for a short time. In spite of the fact that I am afraid of flying, I would like to be a bat.*

Angela: *Even though Paula . . .* (and so on)

Activity 14   *Use It!*

Write down five of the sentences about five different students from Activity 13. Rewrite at least three of them by changing the adverb clause to a prepositional phrase with *in spite of* or *despite*.

Examples:

Even though Brian is afraid of flying, he would like to be a bat.

In spite of his fear of flying, Brian would like to be a bat.

 Lesson 4

Adverb Clauses Showing Purpose

Points to Remember •

❶ The connector *so that* indicates a **purpose** or **goal**. In sentence a., the Coast Guard's goal is to prevent Sarah from reaching the aliens before Larry does.

   a. The Coast Guard is surrounding Sarah **so that** she cannot get to the aliens' ship before Larry.

   b. Raltch studied Earth's languages before leaving home **so that** he would be able to communicate with people.

❷ Notice the use of tenses in purpose clauses:

simple
past
tense

   a. Before leaving home, Raltch **studied** Earth's languages every day so that he **would be** able to communicate with people.
      after-
      past
      tense[1]

      all-time
      tense[2]

   b. Raltch **studies** Earth languages on the spaceship every day so that he **will be** able to communicate with people.
      future
      tense

---

[1] Another name for this tense is *future-in-the-past*. *Would* is the past of *will*.
[2] Another name for this tense is *simple present*.

Activity 15   *Practice It!*

Choose the best verb for each item. Then put it in the correct tense and voice. Use active and passive voices.

grow	repeat	choose	fall
✓ have	save	obey	✓ buy
play	know	be	see

Examples:

Some people take dangerous assignments so that they _____*will have*_____ good stories to tell their children.

The company reduced the price of its products so that more of them __*would be bought*__.

1. Raltch started sending songs to Earth so that the whales _____ they were coming.

2. The government held a lottery for the scientists that wanted to go with Larry so that a small number could _____ fairly.

3. Sarah is working hard so that the Earth's animals _____ her.

4. When she was six, Sarah once tied a piece of string across the top of the basement stairs so that her brother _____ .

5. The lights in Larry's lab are turned off at night so that electricity can _____ .

6. Farmers use fertilizers so that their crops _____ better.

7. The director is writing a memo to all the employees so that Mr. Appleton's terrible mistake _____ not _____ .

8. The couple put their cleaning products on the top shelf yesterday so that their little girl _____ not _____ with them.

9. Mom put a blanket on Jimmy's bed last night so that he _____ warm.

10. The committee gave the film an "R" rating so that it _____ not _____ by young children without their parents' permission.

Activity 16   *Practice It!*

Match a strong main clause on the left with a cause or purpose clause on the right. Then combine the two clauses with *because* or *so that,* depending on the meaning.

Examples:

Main clauses

1. Larry applied for a grant.
2. Paula started swimming with dolphins.

Dependent ideas

✓ a. He could get money for his research.
✓ b. These marine mammals interested her.

1. Larry applied for a grant so that he could get money for his research.

2. Paula started swimming with dolphins because these marine mammals interested her.

Group 1

Main clauses

1. The State requires people to wear seat belts in their cars.
2. Barry is concerned about Paula.
3. The Tuckers have just bought a new freezer.

Dependent ideas

a. They want to keep vegetables from their garden all year long.
b. He loves her.
c. The number of traffic deaths will be reduced.

Group 2

Main clauses

4. Mr. Hill put his glasses on.
5. Bridgit turned down the TV.
6. Paula is giving Sarah false information.
7. The State requires people to wear seat belts in their cars.

Dependent ideas

a. Research shows that the number of traffic deaths can be reduced in this way.
b. Her roommate wanted to study.
c. She will go to the wrong place.
d. He would be able to see the creatures inside the craft.

Group 3

Main clauses

8. Sarah bought a radio telescope.
9. Norma wears green a lot.
10. Some people think that in 1957 the U.S. government classified certain documents "top-secret."

Dependent ideas

a. Nobody would find out that an alien spaceship had crashed in Nebraska.
b. It's her boy friend's favorite color.
c. She could monitor the aliens' signals.

Points to Remember: Expressing Purpose with *In Order To* · · · · · · · · · · · · · · · · · · ·

❶ *In order to* + the simple form of a verb can be used to express purpose.

    a. Larry applied for a grant **in order to get** money for his research.

    b. Paula swam with dolphins **in order to learn** more about these attractive animals.

❷ The words *in order* are often omitted.

    a. **Correct:** Larry applied for a grant **to** get money for his research.

    b. **Correct:** Larry applied for a grant **in order to** get money for his research.

Activity 17   *Practice It!*

Rewrite each sentence using *in order to* (or just *to*). If words are given in parentheses, as in the second example below, use them in your answer.

Examples:

Students sometimes wear charms so that they will do well on tests.

Students sometimes wear charms in order to do well on tests.

Raltch has been studying human languages so that humans will be able to understand him. (help . . . to)

Raltch has been studying human languages in order to help humans to understand him.

1. The whale will come up to the surface so that it can see the aliens' ship.
2. Barry kept his ship near Sarah's so that he would know what she was doing.
3. Sarah turned the wheel so that her ship would head west. (make her ship)
4. Sarah once locked her brother in a closet so that he would not be able to talk to her. (keep . . . from)
5. A whale has come to the surface so that the aliens can see it easily. (allow . . . to)
6. When Larry was 10, his father bought him a telescope so that Larry would be able to study the night sky. (encourage . . . to)

7. Many people exercise regularly so that they can improve their physical condition.
8. Gerry put on her sunglasses so that nobody would recognize her. (keep people)
9. When I got sleepy last night, I had a cup of coffee so that I could keep studying.
10. Ryan tuned up his car so that it would run better. (make)

Points to Remember: Some Punctuation Rules ....

❶ On page 19, you saw two-part compound subjects and two-part compound predicates. No comma is used to separate the two parts of these structures.

   a. **Barry** and **Paula** will be getting married soon.

   b. They are going to **get married** and **raise a family.**

❷ The same is true for any two similar structures: two adjectives, two prepositional phrases, two adverbs, etc.

   a. Paula is **pretty** and **intelligent.**

   b. Sarah would like to have power **on Earth** and **in space.**

❸ When there are three or more similar items in a series, however, they are separated by commas, and the word *and* comes before the last one. If there are three items, there are two commas. If there are four items, there are three commas, and so on.

   a. **Smoch, Blurk,** and **Raltch** will be arriving on Earth soon.

   b. Computers are used **at schools, in offices, on planes,** and **in space.**

❹ A **semicolon** can be used to separate two closely related strong clauses if no connector is used. (**Note:** This is quite rare. It should probably not be done more than once in a five-paragraph composition.)

   a. Barry was an excellent student**;** he got excellent grades.
                  semi-
                  colon

   b. Whales are mammals**;** they breathe air and give birth to their young live.

❺ Semicolons are sometimes used with transitions like *in addition* and *on the other hand.* Periods are much more common before these transitions, however. Commas are used after the transitions.

   a. **Correct:** Barry was very popular with the other students; in addition, he graduated at the top of his class.

   b. **Correct:** Barry was very popular with the other students. In addition, he graduated at the top of his class.

❻ One of the most common mistakes that international students make is to write two strong clauses with only a comma between them. This is called a **comma splice.** See example c. below.

   a. **Correct:** Barry was an excellent student. He got excellent grades.

   b. **Correct:** Barry was an excellent student; he got excellent grades.

   c. **Incorrect:** Barry was an excellent student, he got excellent grades.

Activity 18   *Practice It!*

Using all the rules of punctuation that you have learned so far, punctuate the following items correctly. Do not use semicolons. Do not change any words.

Example:

Barry has been doing fine work for the Coast Guard consequently he hopes to be promoted soon much depends on the success of Project Alien

Barry has been doing fine work for the Coast Guard. Consequently, he hopes to be promoted soon. Much depends on the success of Project Alien.

1. Smoch Blurk and Raltch will soon be arriving on Earth so all the world's scientists are focusing their attention on a location in the Pacific Ocean

2. Paula hopes to succeed but she may fail

3. Larry's ship is being used for complex scientific research so it is filled with expensive equipment

4. Paula sat down turned on the computer and entered the password to the Coast Guard Network she quickly got access to many top government secrets

5. Some people believe that aliens have come to Earth many times and helped people with certain enormous projects like the pyramids in Egypt they say that the Egyptians could never have built the pyramids without help from aliens

6. A female dolphin can have only one baby a year the whole species is limited by this reality as a result other females stay near a mother and her infant they protect it and make sure it doesn't swim too far away

7. Many international students are Moslems therefore they read food labels carefully to be sure that the products do not contain pork or ham

8. Alfredo loves sailing so he was excited to find out about the sailing club on campus he went to a meeting last week and met a number of other students with similar interests the members of the club have agreed to buy an old sailboat together repair it paint it and take it out on the lake

9. The little girl fell and skinned her knee so she started to cry her mother came to comfort her and soon the child was calm again

10. Chong Sing has watched North American students playing with Frisbees many times but he still doesn't know how to throw one himself he hopes to learn soon the sport looks like fun

Activity 19 *Use It!*

Beings from another planet will soon arrive on Earth! Imagine that you are your country's ambassador to the United Nations. You need to give a speech to the General Assembly giving your country's official position on the arrival of the aliens. As the ambassador to the U.N., what will you say? Does your country want to welcome the aliens? Does your country want to prepare to fight? Write between 250 and 300 words. Your teacher will tell you which of the following sentence types you need to include in your speech. Underline the special sentences, and label them by letter so that your teacher can find them easily.

a. a simple sentence

b. a compound sentence with *but* or *so*

c. a compound sentence with *nor*

d. a complex sentence with *even though*

e. a complex sentence with *by the time* or *as long as*

f. a reduced time clause

g. a sentence with *because* or *due to the fact that*

h. a sentence with *because of*

i. a prepositional phrase beginning with *in spite of*

j. a sentence with *so . . . that* or *such . . . that*

k. a sentence with *so that*

l. a sentence with *in order to*

Example:

Good evening, ladies and gentlemen:

(e) By the time this General Assembly meets again, we will have met beings from another planet! The President of my country has asked me to talk to you tonight about the arrival of the alien spaceship. (a) The alien's planet is certainly very different from our own. This means . . .

Chapter 8

ADVENTURES AT CAMELOT
LEARNING THE STORY

Activity 1   *Get the Background!*

Look at the story square on page 88, and read this introduction.

"Adventures at Camelot" is the legend, or popular traditional story, of King Arthur, an English leader who lived many centuries ago. There are four main characters in this legend: Arthur, the king; Guinevere, a beautiful and generous lady; Mordred, a nasty young man; and Lancelot, an almost perfect knight.[1] A minor character[2] is the magician Merlin. (You can see him in Picture 1). Finally, the Round Table is not a character, but it, too, is an important part of the story.

"Adventures at Camelot" is the story of one man's dream of a country where men and women would behave perfectly. In Arthur's perfect country, men would be brave, courteous,[3] and honest. They would be loyal[4] to their ladies—and to their king. Women would be beautiful and virtuous.[5] The leaders of this country would sit at a round table, that is, a table with no head, where all would be equal. In Arthur's dream, he and his knights would make decisions together. The knights of the Round Table would always do the right thing.

Arthur failed to achieve his dream; the men and women of Camelot did not behave perfectly. One reason for the failure was a love triangle. As you know, "perfect" behavior is unusual when two men love the same woman. Furthermore, the knights of the Round Table were not always honest and loyal.

Yes, some terrible things happened in Camelot. Your job is to figure out what went wrong.

Vocabulary

[1] a knight: a gentleman-soldier
[2] a minor character: a less important person in a story
[3] courteous: polite in a generous and helpful way
[4] loyal: faithful, always doing their duty in supporting their ladies and their king
[5] virtuous: with excellent thoughts and behavior

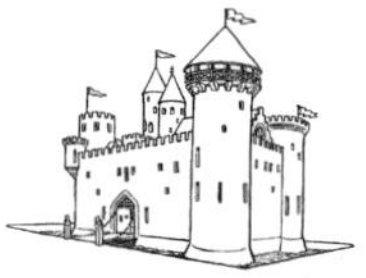

Adventures at Camelot

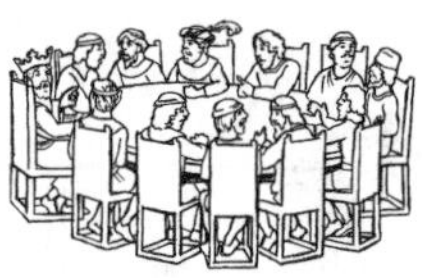

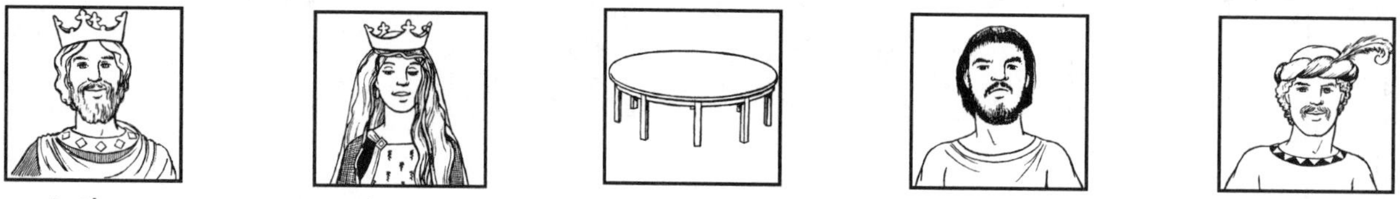

Arthur | Guinevere | The Round Table | Mordred | Lancelot

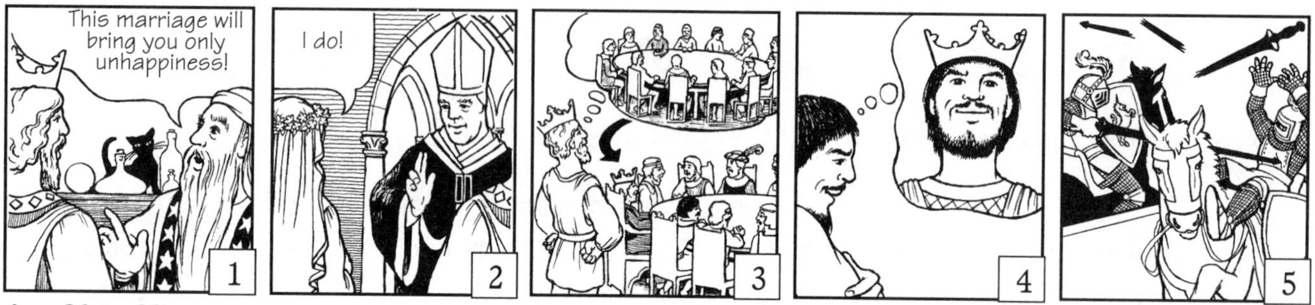
This marriage will bring you only unhappiness!
1
I do!
2
3
4
5

Age 30 to 33

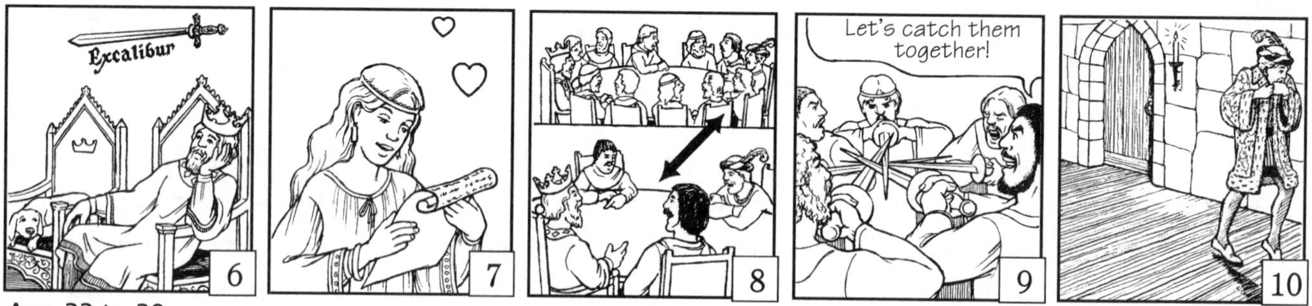
Excalibur
6
7
8
Let's catch them together!
9
10

Age 33 to 39

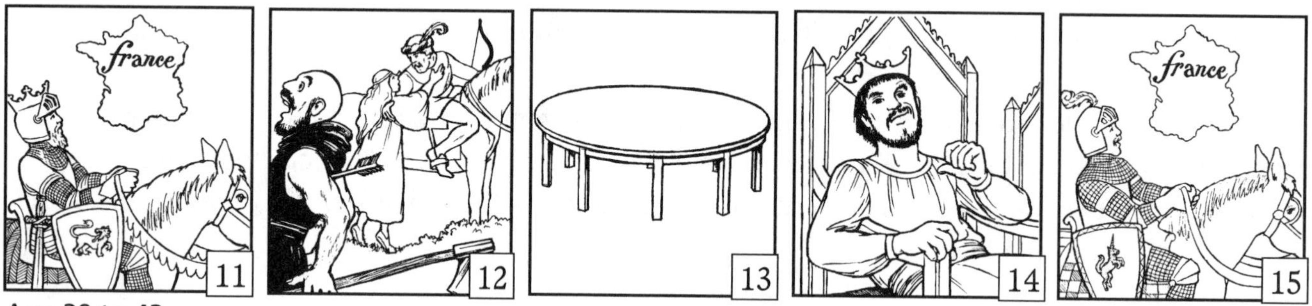
france
11
12
13
14
france
15

Age 39 to 43

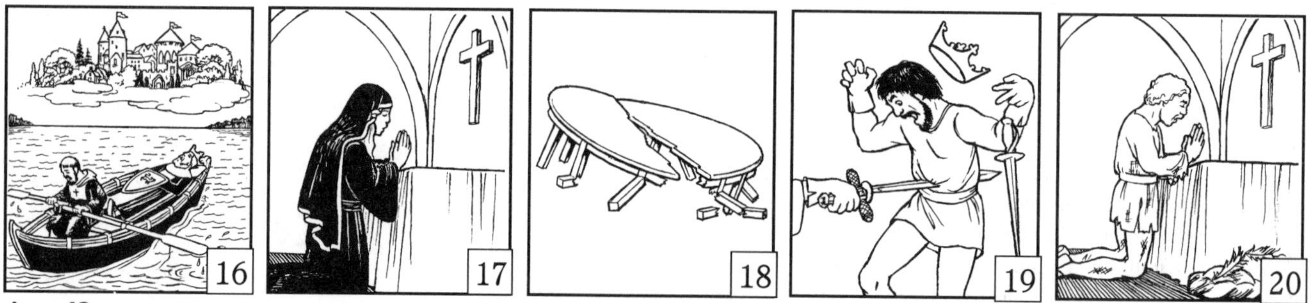
16
17
18
19
20

Age 43

Activity 2   *Get More Facts!*

Read these major points about the story as you study the pictures. The numbers refer to
Arthur's age in each row of pictures.

From age 30 to 33:

Picture 1:   The magician Merlin advised Arthur not to marry as he had planned.

Picture 2:   Guinevere was married in a very big wedding.

Picture 3:   In A.D. 525, the Round Table was just a dream in the mind of King Arthur. By
A.D. 528, it had become a reality with twelve knights.

Picture 4:   Mordred dreamed of becoming king.

Picture 5:   Lancelot arrived and quickly became Camelot's most famous knight.

From age 33 to 39:

Picture 6:   Unhappy Arthur spent a lot of time alone.

Picture 7:   Guinevere sometimes received romantic notes.

Picture 8:   The knights began to fight among themselves. One by one, they left the
Round Table.

Picture 9:   Mordred arrived in Camelot and made friends.

Picture 10: Lancelot often had to tiptoe[1] around the castle.[2]

From age 39 to 43:

(**Note:** These pictures are not in the correct order from left to right. When you figure
out the correct order, you will understand the story better.)

Picture 11: Arthur went to France.

Picture 12: Guinevere was rescued at the last possible moment and taken to safety.

Picture 13: The Round Table was deserted.[3]

Picture 14: Mordred made himself king.

Picture 15: Lancelot suddenly left England for France.

Vocabulary

[1] to tiptoe: to walk very quietly on the ends of one's toes
[2] a castle: a home of a king or other powerful person. Castles often have thick, strong walls for protection.
[3] deserted: left with no people

Age 43:

Picture 16: Arthur was taken to the island of Avalon to recover from injuries.

Picture 17: Guinevere became a nun.[1]

Picture 18: The Round Table was deserted and broken.

Picture 19: Mordred was killed in battle.

Picture 20: Lancelot gave up his adventurous life and started a life of prayer.

Activity 3   *Discuss It!*

You have read some of the major points about the story, but there is still a lot that you don't know. In small groups, discuss these questions:

1. Do you have any ideas about the relationships, or connections, between the characters?

2. What more do you need to know to understand the story completely?

Activity 4   *Learn the Whole Story!*

Write one or two *yes/no* questions that you can ask your teacher to learn more about "Adventures at Camelot." Ask your teacher your questions. Ask as many questions as you think you need to understand the story completely.

Examples:

Student 1: *In Picture 7, did the letter come from Mordred?*

Teacher: No, it didn't.

Student 2: *In Picture 14, was Mordred a good king?*

Teacher: No, he wasn't.

Vocabulary

[1] a nun: a member of an organization of women that spend their whole lives in religious service

Activity 5   *Double-Check It!*

Listen as your teacher reads each question. Then write the question and check (✔) the best answer.

Example:

Teacher: Why did Lancelot come to Camelot?

Students write: *Why did Lancelot come to Camelot?*

a. ☐ To become king.

b. ✔ To become a knight of the Round Table.

c. ☐ To learn magic from Merlin.

1. _____

_____

   a. ☐ Arthur.   b. ☐ Nobody.   c. ☐ Lancelot.

2. _____

_____

   a. ☐ The other knight was his enemy.

   b. ☐ He wanted to prove that he was the best knight.

   c. ☐ The other knight was Arthur, and Lancelot was trying to kill him.

3. _____

   a. ☐ Lancelot.   b. ☐ Mordred.   c. ☐ Arthur.

4. _____

   a. ☐ Get more people to oppose Arthur.

   b. ☐ Form a sword-fighting team.

   c. ☐ Create a second Round Table.

5. _____

   a. ☐ Lancelot.   b. ☐ Mordred.   c. ☐ Arthur.

6. _____

   a. ☐ They preferred a more traditional rectangular table.

   b. ☐ They all knew about Guinevere's love affair with Lancelot and were upset about it.

   c. ☐ Merlin had convinced them that they could make more money in another country.

7. _____

   a. ☐ She had stolen some of King Arthur's gold and jewels.

   b. ☐ Mordred sentenced her to death because she refused to marry him.

   c. ☐ Arthur sentenced her to death because she was unfaithful to him.

8. _____

   a. ☐ Arthur.   b. ☐ Guinevere.   c. ☐ Lancelot.

9. _____

_____

   a. ☐ They wanted to show Arthur the best way to live.

   b. ☐ They were sorry for their past actions and knew that they could not continue their love affair.

   c. ☐ They felt that they could get the most political power that way.

10. _____

   a. ☐ Avalon.   b. ☐ Camelot.   c. ☐ It's unclear.

Chapter 9

ADJECTIVE CLAUSES   PART 1

 **Lesson 1**

Adjective Clauses: The Basics

Points to Remember •

❶ In the examples below, the adjective clauses[1] are in **dark** letters.

    a. Arthur was a king **who tried to build a perfect society.**

    b. Many knights had the same idea **Arthur had.**

    c. The Round Table, **which was Arthur's dream,** lasted several years.

    d. For a few years, Camelot really was a place **where men and women tried to do the right things.**

    e. Arthur may still be on the magical island **that he was taken to after his battle with Mordred.**

❷ Here are three facts about adjective clauses:

    • An adjective clause often begins with a connector like *who, where,* or *that.*[2] The connector *that* can sometimes be omitted.

    • Every adjective clause is a complete weak clause with a subject and a verb.

    • Almost every adjective clause modifies, or gives information about, a noun or pronoun before it. This noun or pronoun is usually (but not always) directly before the adjective clause.

---

[1] Adjective clauses are also called *relative clauses.*
[2] The words *that, which, whom,* and *who* are relative pronouns. *Whose* is a relative possessive adjective when it is used in an adjective clause.

❸ The following examples illustrate the three facts in Point 2.

                                S   —— V ——

    a. Arthur was a king **who** **tried to build a perfect society**.

                              connector

- The connector is *who*.

- The subject of the adjective clause is *who*. The complete verb of the adjective clause is *tried to build*.

- The adjective clause modifies the noun *king* before it.

                                               S   V

    b. Many knights had the same idea **Arthur had**.

- There is no connector. (The connector *that* has been omitted.)

- The subject of the adjective clause is *Arthur*. The verb of the adjective clause is *had*.

- The adjective clause modifies the noun *idea* before it.

❹ Sometimes an adjective clause modifies an idea or a fact.

    Lancelot came from France to join the Round Table, which pleased Arthur very much.

    (*Which* = an idea = that Lancelot came from France to join the Round Table)

Activity 1   *Analyze It!*

Underline the adjective clause in each sentence. Box the word(s) it modifies. Mark the subject and verb of the adjective clause. If there is a connector, underline it a second time.

Examples:

                                                                     S   V

The Round Table was the key to the |kind of government| that Arthur wanted.

                                                           S   V

The British and the French have constructed a |tunnel| that connects their two countries.

1.   Arthur went to France to catch the man who had been sending notes to his queen.

2.   Arthur had a magical sword that protected him from injury.

3.   The knights sat at a table that had no head.

4.   Mordred and some friends caught Lancelot and Guinevere together, which forced Arthur to punish the two lovers.

5. The man Arthur followed had been his favorite knight.

6. A story very similar to the one you have learned was used as the plot for a popular musical play and movie called *Camelot*.

7. Wyoming, which is a state in the northwest of the United States, is famous for its fantastic scenery.

8. A widow is a woman whose husband has died.

9. The computers the company bought in the 1980s completely changed the office's operations.

10. Zeus, who was the supreme god in ancient Greek religion, was believed to control heaven and Earth.

 Lesson 2

Structure-S and Structure-O Adjective Clauses

Points to Remember: Structure-S Adjective Clauses ·························

❶ Adjective clauses have two basic structures: Structure-S and Structure-O. In Structure-S clauses, the connector is the subject. The word *that*[1] can usually be used as the connector.

                                                        S   V

a. For years, Arthur loved and respected the knights *that* **sat with him** at the Round Table.

                                 S ——— V———

b. The magical sword *that* **was hanging over Arthur's throne** was called *Excalibur*.

❷ The verb in a Structure-S clause must agree with the word that the clause modifies.

                                         S ——— V———

a. Arthur was never very close to the **nephew** that **was trying** to become king.

(The singular verb *was trying* agrees with *nephew*.)

                  S V

b. **People** that **try** to be perfect all the time cannot succeed.

(The plural verb *try* agrees with *people*.)

---

[1] The words *who, which, whom, whose, where, when*, and *why* are also sometimes possible. You will study them in Chapter 10.

❸ Do not double the subject in a Structure–S adjective clause.

The magician that ~~he~~ helped Arthur was extremely old.

Activity 2   *Practice It!*

Combine the two sentences into one by changing the second sentence to an adjective clause.

> **Example:**
>
> Arthur lived in a castle. The castle was designed by the greatest British architect of the fifth century.
>
> *Arthur lived in a castle that was designed by the greatest British architect of the fifth century.*

1. The king had a horse. This horse could run like the wind.

2. Arthur wanted people to solve their differences by discussing them. These people disagreed with each other.

3. All the knights were supposed to respect the decisions. These decisions were made at the Round Table.

4. The people made many changes in the story. These people told the story over the centuries.

5. The woman narrowly escaped death. This woman was saved by Lancelot.

6. A refrigerator may use too much electricity. This refrigerator costs less in the store.

7. If you buy a used car, be sure to get a used car. This car has been maintained regularly.

8. People tell similar stories about a bright light at the end of a long tunnel. These people have had near death experiences.

9. The word "tanker" refers to a ship. This ship transports oil.

10. Do you know the name of the queen? This queen was ruling England in 1850.

Points to Remember: Structure-O Adjective Clauses ·························

❶ In Structure–O adjective clauses, the connector is not the subject of the adjective clause. It is the object. The word *that* can usually be used as the connector.

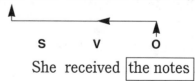

a. Guinevere always destroyed the notes ***that*** **she received from Lancelot.**

(The connector *that* = the notes)

b. One of the most dangerous sports

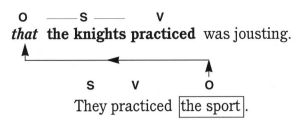

O   —S—   V
that **the knights practiced** was jousting.

S   V   O
They practiced the sport .

(The connector *that* = one of the sports)

❷ Do not double the object in a Structure–O adjective clause:

The castle that Arthur and Guinevere lived in ̶i̶t̶ was cold in the winter.

Activity 3   *Analyze It!*

Underline the adjective clause in each sentence. Label its subject, verb, and object.
(**Note:** Some adjective clauses have no object.) State whether it is Structure-S or Structure-O.

Examples:

            O *S* *V*
Guinevere had birds that she used for hunting. *(Structure-O)*

       S   *V*
The people that advise modern leaders must understand today's world. *(Structure–S)*

1. The horse that Arthur rode to France was light brown.

2. When Mordred became king, there were few people that remained loyal to Arthur.

3. Arthur could never have imagined some of the technology that makes our lives comfortable today.

4. Squirrels are responsible for planting many of the trees that grow in England's forests.

5. Much of the land that farmers grow crops on today was forest in Arthur's time.

6. Would you like to live in a castle like the one that Arthur and Guinevere lived in?

Activity 4   *Practice It!*

In each group, match each question on the left with the idea on the right about the same subject. Then answer each question by writing a sentence with an adjective clause beginning with *that* and including the idea on the right. (**Note:** Begin your sentence with the word in parentheses.) Finally, decide whether the adjective clause is Structure–S or Structure–O.

Examples:

Questions	Related Ideas
1. Which horse was the fastest? (The horse . . .)	a. Arthur and Guinevere lived in it.
2. Which castle was cold in the winter? (The castle . . .)	b. It carried Lancelot to France.

1. *The horse that carried Lancelot to France was the fastest. (Structure-S)*

2. *The castle that Arthur and Guinevere lived in was cold in the winter. (Structure-O)*

Group 1

Questions	Related Ideas
1. Which man spent a lot of time alone? (The man . . .)	a. Guinevere wore it.
2. Which woman was Lancelot in love with? (Lancelot . . .)	b. He established the Round Table.
3. Which crown had seventy jewels in it? (The crown . . .)	c. Arthur made her his queen.

Group 2

Questions	Related Ideas
4. Which man could see into the future? (The man . . .)	a. It was given to Guinevere in jail.
5. Which hat did Lancelot wear? (Lancelot . . .)	b. His brother gave it to him.
6. Which food was not very good? (The food . . .)	c. He had a long, grey beard.

Group 3

Questions

7. Which sword did Arthur always carry in battle? (Arthur . . . OR In battle, . . .)

8. Which couple felt very confused? (The couple . . .)

9. Which table was the symbol of the new government? (The table . . .)

10. Which man made a special trip to Camelot? (The man . . .)

Related Ideas

a. Guinevere's father gave it to Arthur.

b. It protected him from all danger.

c. He married Arthur and Guinevere.

d. They had to meet secretly.

Activity 5   *Use It!*

Step 1: Work in groups of two or three. Read the six sections of the story "How Arthur Became King" and number them to indicate the correct sequence of events. The first part of the story, Section D, has been numbered for you.

Step 2: Stay in your groups. Write at least eight sentences about the story: four with Structure–S clauses and four with Structure–O clauses. Use only the connector *that*. Underline each adjective clause and label its subject, verb, and object.

Examples:

             S   V   O

The magician that took Arthur to Ector's castle could predict the future. (Structure–S)

             O   S   V

The child that Merlin took to Ector's castle was a prince. (Structure–O)

(**Note:** Your adjective clauses must modify common nouns like magician, child, and knight, not proper nouns like Merlin, Arthur, and Ector. You will learn the reason for this in Chapter 10, Lesson 3.)

Examples:

Correct: *The magician that took Arthur to Ector's castle could predict the future.*

Incorrect: *Merlin that took Arthur to Ector's castle . . .*

How Arthur Became King

Section A: _____

One day, after sixteen years of terrible fighting in Britain, Merlin visited the Archbishop of Canterbury.[1] "Utha's son, the new king, will soon reappear," Merlin told the archbishop. "He will be a great king, and he will reunite Britain." Merlin told the archbishop to invite knights from all over Britain to a great tournament.[2] The new king would be in the crowd.

Sir Ector and his son, Sir Kay, were among the competitors in the tournament. Still too young to compete, Arthur went along to help them.

Section B: _____

The three returned to the stone. Kay put the sword back into the stone, but no matter how hard he pulled, he could not get it out again. Innocently, Arthur said, "I can do it." And he easily pulled the sword out again. Realizing what this meant, Ector and Kay knelt down before their new king.

The news spread quickly. Although at first some of the knights did not like having a beardless boy as their king, the common people quickly accepted Arthur as Utha's son and loved him from the first day of his reign.[3]

Section C: _____

Merlin gave the baby to a good knight named Sir Ector and his wife, Bertoth. Soon after that, Utha died. Without a strong leader, the British knights again fought among themselves, and invaders again came from outside the country to steal and kill.

Ector and Bertoth called the baby Arthur. They loved him and raised him with their own older son, Kay.

Vocabulary

[1] the Archbishop of Canterbury: during the Middle Ages, the head of the Roman Catholic Church in Britain
[2] a tournament: a contest
[3] a reign: the period of time that a king or queen rules a country

Section D: ___1___

From the first century A.D. to the beginning of the fifth century, the Romans controlled Britain. Roman law made this a time of peace, and the people prospered.[1]

By 410 A.D., the Romans had become weak and had to leave Britain. In the absence of a strong government in Britain, invaders[2] attacked from other lands, and the British knights began fighting among themselves. A young prince named Utha, however, was able to stop the fighting in the south. Later, he became king of all Britain and stopped the fighting everywhere.

King Utha and his wife, Igraine, had a baby boy. This should have been a time of great joy, but it was not. The magician Merlin came to Utha and told him: "Utha, you will soon die. Your enemies will want to kill your child. Let me take him! I can take him to a safe place, and he will someday be king." Utha and Igraine sadly agreed, and Merlin took the baby.

Section E: _____

On the way back to the inn[3] to get Kay's sword, Arthur passed the stone with the sword in it. He had not paid attention to the stories about the sword, so he did not recognize it. Nor did he see the words on the stone. Thinking he could borrow the weapon, he easily pulled it from the stone, got back on his horse, and gave it to his older brother. Sir Kay took it immediately from Arthur. Seeing his son with the sword, Ector asked Kay where he had gotten it. He lied: "I pulled it from the stone."

"We must return to the stone so that you can show me," Ector told him.

Section F: _____

When the knights arrived at the tournament, they were amazed to find a large stone with a magnificent, jeweled sword stuck deeply into it. On the stone were written the words: "Whosoever[4] pulls this sword from this stone is the rightful king of Britain."

One by one, Ector, Kay, and every other knight tried to pull the sword from the stone. One by one, they failed.

The tournament began! Sir Kay realized that he had forgotten his sword. "Arthur," he said, "I have forgotten my sword. Go back to our rooms and get it."

Vocabulary

1   to prosper: to succeed and have plenty of money
2   invaders: armies from other countries
3   an inn: a hotel
4   whosoever: whoever, the person that

 **Lesson 3**

More About Structure-O Adjective Clauses

Points to Remember: The Zero-Word ···

❶ The connector *that* is often omitted from Structure-O adjective clauses. In other words, it is often omitted when it is not the subject of the adjective clause.

                                                             S   V

a. **Correct:**   Lancelot was respected by the knights **he defeated.**

                                                                      S   V

b. **Correct:**   Lancelot was respected by the knights **that he defeated.**

                                             S   V

c. **Correct:**   The family **Merlin gave the baby to** treated the child like their own.

                                                      S   V

d. **Correct:**   The family **that Merlin gave the baby to** treated the child like their own.

❷ We can use the symbol Ø to represent the omitted pronoun. We will call the symbol Ø the **zero-word. (Note:** Of course, nobody writes the zero-word normally, but it is useful in grammar books.)

a.   Lancelot was respected by the knights Ø he defeated.

b.   The family Ø Merlin gave the baby to treated the child like their own.

❸ The pronoun *that* can never be omitted from Structure-S adjective clauses.

                                                S   V

a. **Correct:**   Arthur loved the couple **that** brought him up.

b. **Incorrect:** Arthur loved the couple Ø brought him up.

                                              S   V

c. **Correct:**   The sword **that** protected Arthur in battle had been created magically by Merlin.

d. **Incorrect:** The sword Ø protected Arthur in battle had been created magically by Merlin.

Activity 6   *Analyze It!*

First, underline the adjective clause and mark its subject. Then, if the pronoun *that* is not the subject of the adjective clause, cross it out and write the zero-word, Ø, above it. Finally, practice reading the sentences with the zero-word out loud in a natural way.

Examples:

The sword ~~that~~ Arthur pulled from the stone had magical powers.
(Ø above "that", S above "Arthur")

(reading out loud) *The sword Arthur pulled from the stone had magical powers.*

The woman that gave Arthur the sword lived in a lake.
(S above "that")

The word "that" cannot be omitted because it is the subject of the adjective clause.

1. The horses that knights rode had to be fast and strong.
2. During the Middle Ages, European boys from noble families studied the manners that they would have to follow as knights.
3. The code of behavior that knights followed was called "chivalry."
4. A knight that did not honor women was not respected.
5. A knight was expected to serve a noble lady that he might never even see in person.
6. Merlin had powers that allowed him to "remember" the future.
7. Guinevere was very upset by the situation that she found herself in.
8. The two men that loved her were best friends.
9. This was not the kind of problem that could be solved in a day.

10. The only solution that Guinevere could think of was for Lancelot to leave Camelot, and that would have been unbearable.

Point to Remember: Prepositions at the Ends of Structure-O Clauses ··········

Some Structure-O adjective clauses end with a preposition. This preposition is necessary to the meaning of the sentence. (**Note:** Parentheses around a word indicate that it can be omitted.)

  a. The table (that) the knights sat **at** was round.
     (The knights sat **at** the table.)

  b. The feather (that) Lancelot wrote **with** came from his favorite falcon.
     (Lancelot wrote **with** the falcon feather.)

Activity 7　*Practice It!*

Combine the two sentences into one by changing the second sentence to an adjective clause. Remember the preposition in each adjective clause. Omit the word *that* if you like, or keep it.

Examples:

The castle was cold in the winter. Arthur lived in the castle.

The castle that Arthur lived in was cold in the winter.

The event was the discovery of an ancient city. The archaeologists were excited about the event.

The event the archaeologists were excited about was the discovery of an ancient city.

1. Arthur was married to the woman. Lancelot was in love with the woman.
2. The people found the king. They were looking for the king.
3. Arthur was not born into the family. He grew up in the family.
4. The problem was not easily solved. The knights were upset about the problem.
5. The England was very different from today's England. King Arthur lived in the England.[1]
6. According to chivalry, a knight might never even see the noble lady. He devoted his life to the noble lady.

7. The room was small and cold. The patient had to wait for the doctor in the room.
8. The old man often visited the tree. He had carved his initials in the tree as a boy.
9. The cage is only ten feet by ten feet. That lion is kept in the cage.
10. Helping young artists is the goal of the organization. Ms. Smith is a member of that organization.

---

[1] Normally, the word *the* is not used before country names. This is a very special case: *the England* means *England at a specific time in history.*

Activity 8   *Use It!*

Working in a group of three or four, find or draw one or more pictures of people doing interesting things. Write at least eight sentences with Structure–O adjective clauses about the picture. All of the sentences must include the zero-word (Ø), and at least three of the adjective clauses must end with a preposition. Write the symbol Ø in each sentence. Underline the adjective clauses once and the prepositions twice. (**Note:** Don't be shy about drawing! The person who drew the picture below obviously has no artistic talent. Anybody can draw!)

Examples:

The balls <u>Ø the man is juggling</u> can't be very heavy.

The tower <u>Ø the woman is standing <u>on</u></u> is probably made of wood.

ADJECTIVE CLAUSES PART 2

 Lesson 1

The Connector Whose

Points to Remember ···

❶ The connector *whose* indicates possession, that is, that something or somebody "belongs"[1] to somebody or something. Structure–S clauses with *whose* are more common than Structure–O clauses.

Examples with Structure–S:

a. Soon after becoming king, Arthur saw a young

     ——— S ———   V

woman *whose* **beauty made his heart beat faster.**

b. A young woman *whose* **family owned a great deal of land** married the king.

Examples with Structure–O:

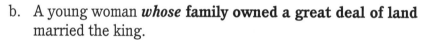

              ——— O ——— S   V

a. Arthur was happy to find a queen *whose* **family he respected.**

b. A friend *whose* **opinion Arthur respected** advised the young king against the marriage.

❷ In both structures, the word *whose* comes between two nouns. These three words make up the **whose group.** In every *whose* group, the noun on the right "belongs" to the noun on the left.

---

[1] The word *belongs* is in quotation marks here because people do not belong to other people, but a noun referring to a person can follow the word *whose.*

Arthur saw a young | woman whose beauty | made his heart beat faster.

The *whose* group = *woman whose beauty*

The beauty "belongs" to the woman.

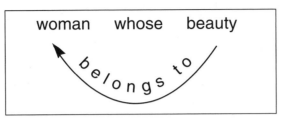

The Whose Group

❸ The word *whose* can refer to things or people. In the example below, the word *whose* refers to the sword.

> After Arthur's first sword was destroyed, he received another **sword whose magic powers** protected him.
> (The magic powers belonged to the sword.)

Activity 1   *Practice It!*

In each item, combine the two sentences using an adjective clause beginning with *whose*. State whether the adjective clause is Structure–S or Structure–O.

Example:

Arthur saw a young woman. Her beauty made his heart beat faster.

Arthur saw a young woman whose beauty made his heart beat faster. (Structure–S)

1. A young man became the new king. His father had died sixteen years before.
2. The woman felt very unhappy. Her husband had put her in jail.
3. Arthur was often helped by a strange man. The strange man's laboratory contained many mysterious things.
4. An historian will be speaking at the student union tonight. The historian's specialty is the Middle Ages.
5. Mordred was the nephew of the king. He wanted the king's crown.
6. Arthur lived in a castle. The walls of the castle could stop almost any enemy.

7. Cattle are animals. People use these animals' skins to make shoes.
8. An orphan is a child. His or her parents have died.
9. Ms. Hananto called the police about a neighbor. This neighbor's dog had chased Ms. Hananto's daughter.
10. The neighbor gave her pet away. Ms. Hananto had complained about the neighbor's dog.

Activity 2 — *Practice It!*

This is a review of the adjective clause structures that you have studied so far. In each item, combine the two sentences by changing the second sentence to an adjective clause beginning with *that, whose,* or the zero-word Ø. Use Ø whenever possible. Make changes in nouns and pronouns where necessary. Keep your paper. You'll need it later.

Example:

The boy became king. He pulled the sword from the stone.

The boy that pulled the sword from the stone became king.

1. Many knights were unhappy to have a new king. The new king looked so young.

2. Many knights were unhappy to have a new king. They knew so little about him.

3. Many knights were unhappy to have a new king. His background was a mystery.

4. Many knights were unhappy to have a new king. They didn't know his background.

5. A new king must prove himself. He looks very young.

6. A new king must prove himself. His background is a mystery.

7. A new king must prove himself. The people don't know his background.

8. A new king must prove himself. The people know little about him.

9. When Arthur pulled the sword from the stone, the people couldn't believe their eyes. The people saw him do it.

10. However, a magician appeared and gave a speech. The people feared and respected the magician.

11. The magician said that the boy was Utha's son. They saw the boy in front of them.

12. The boy was Utha's son. They doubted the boy's identity.

13. The boy was the rightful king. The boy had drawn the sword from the stone.

14. Arthur soon proved himself by leading an army against the invaders. The invaders had controlled parts of Britain for years.

15. Arthur forced the invaders to leave Britain. He defeated the invaders.

16. The man was the king. His wife loved another.

17. A rain forest is being cut down for agriculture. The rain forest's soil is very poor.

18. The queen was angered by the pictures. These pictures were taken of her at the ceremony.

19. The Mayans developed a number system. This number system allowed the Mayans to do calculations easily.

20. The number system permitted the Mayans to do calculations easily. The Mayans developed this number system.

Activity 3 | *Use It!*

Return to Activity 5 on page 99, in which you wrote sentences with adjective clauses based on the story "How Arthur Became King." Write at least four more sentences about the story. Each sentence must include an adjective clause with *whose*.

Example:

Merlin visited the king whose son had to be protected.

 **Lesson 2**

The Connectors Where, When, *and* Why

Points to Remember ·

❶ Adjective clauses can begin with *where, when,* and *why.*[1]

                                             S   V

   a.   The period of history **when** Arthur lived is called the Middle Ages.

                                    S   V

   b.   Lancelot rescued Guinevere from the place **where** she was about to die for her love affair with the Frenchman.

                                 S   V

   c.   Arthur looked very young. That is one reason **why** the knights were not happy that he was their new king.

❷ A complete clause (S + V) always follows the connectors *where, when,* and *why.* Example b. below is wrong because there is no complete clause after the connector *where.*

                                    S   V

   a. **Correct:**   Merlin had a cave where **he did** many experiments.

   b. **Incorrect:** Merlin had a cave where had many experiments.

---

[1] The connectors *where, when,* and *why* are traditionally called *relative adverbs.*

Activity 4 *Practice It!*

In each item, combine the sentences. Use an adjective clause beginning with *when, where,* or *why* in each item.

Examples:

Camelot was a land. People tried to behave perfectly in that land.

Camelot was a land where people tried to behave perfectly.

Spring is a time of year. Many people fall in love at that time of year.

Spring is a time of year when many people fall in love.

Guinevere was beautiful. That was the reason. Arthur fell in love with her for that reason.

Guinevere was beautiful. That was the reason why Arthur fell in love with her.

1. January in Camelot was a month. People stayed close to their fires during that month.
2. The stadium was a place. Knights practiced jousting in that place.
3. Jousting was dangerous. That is the reason. Many knights were seriously injured in tournaments.
4. Morning was the time of day. Arthur liked to go hunting at that time of day.
5. Many young men's brains are injured in the boxing ring. That is the reason. Many people want to outlaw boxing.
6. Greece is the country. The first Olympic Games were held in that country.

Activity 5 *Use It!*

Below you will see a list of times and places. Choose ten of them. What happens in these places? What happens at these times? For each item, make a sentence with an adjective clause beginning with *where* or *when*.

Examples:

childhood   *Childhood is a time when people have few responsibilities.*

kitchens   *Kitchens are rooms where people prepare their food.*

babyhood	the ocean	New Year's Day
restaurants	winter	deserts
Sundays	laboratories	castles
the language lab	birthdays	prisons
Fridays	Halloween	forests

Activity 6   *Use It!*

Choose ten of the sentences below. Write a second sentence for each one beginning with the words "That is the reason why . . . ."

Example:

Arthur was honest and brave.

That is the reason why his people loved him.

1. Mordred wanted to become king.

2. Lancelot was a fine jouster.

3. Doctors in Arthur's time knew very little about the human body.

4. There were no telecommunications in Arthur's time.

5. Horses were the fastest means of transportation in Arthur's day.

6. Michael has to hand in a ten-page research paper today.

7. Oranges supply vitamin C.

8. The school's football team scored the winning goal.

9. The library has newspapers from all over the world.

10. The XYZ Corporation produces excellent stereo equipment.

11. Elephants are becoming rarer and rarer.

12. There is no water on the moon.

Lesson 3

Essential vs. Extra-Info Adjective Clauses

Point to Remember: The Other Connectors for Adjective Clauses ··············

The connectors *that* and *Ø* can be used in many adjective clauses, but other connectors are also possible.[1] Study the chart and the examples below.

	People	Things
Subject	1 that who	2 that (which)[2]
Not Subject	3 Ø that (whom) [who][3]	4 Ø that (which)

a. **Box 1:** The knights knew nothing about the boy $\left\{ \begin{array}{c} \textbf{that} \\ \textbf{who} \end{array} \right\}$ pulled the sword from the stone.

   (The connector refers to a person, Arthur, and is the subject of the adjective clause. Therefore, we can use the connectors in box 1.)

b. **Box 2:** Merlin had a special box $\left\{ \begin{array}{c} \textbf{that} \\ \textbf{which} \end{array} \right\}$ contained his most important materials.

   (The connector refers to a thing and is the subject of the adjective clause. Therefore, we can use the connectors from box 2. *That* is usually preferred.)

c. **Box 3:** The king $\left\{ \begin{array}{c} \textbf{Ø} \\ \textbf{that} \\ \textbf{(whom)} \\ \textbf{[who]} \end{array} \right\}$ Mordred hoped to dethrone invited over a hundred

   knights to sit with him at his Round Table.

   (The connector refers to a person and is not the subject of the adjective clause. Therefore, the connectors from box 3 above are used. *That* and *Ø* are usually preferred.)

---

[1] *Whose, where,* and *when* can also be used in both essential and extra-info adjective clauses.

[2] The parentheses around *which* in boxes 2 and 4 and around *who* in box 3 indicate that these connectors are possible but not usually preferred.

[3] In informal language, *who* can be used in this way. In formal language, this use of *who* is unacceptable.

d. **Box 4:** The speech $\left\{ \begin{array}{c} \varnothing \\ \textbf{that} \\ \textbf{(which)} \end{array} \right\}$ Merlin gave helped to establish Arthur as the true king.

(The connector refers to a thing and is not the subject of the adjective clause. Therefore, we can use the connectors in box 4. *That* and *Ø* are usually preferred.)

Activity 7   *Practice It!*

Return to Activity 2 on page 108 and indicate all possible connectors.

Example:

The boy became king. He pulled the sword from the stone.

The boy $\left\{ \begin{array}{c} \textbf{\textit{that}} \\ \textbf{\textit{who}} \end{array} \right\}$ *pulled the sword from the stone became king.*

Points to Remember: Essential and Extra-Info Adjective Clauses · · · · · · · · · · · · ·

❶ All the adjective clauses you have studied so far are **essential adjective clauses**. Essential adjective clauses help to identify the noun or pronoun that they are modifying. Sometimes, omitting an essential adjective clause makes the meaning of a sentence unclear or untrue.

  a. **Unclear:** The man didn't often sleep very well.

  (Which man? Merlin? Mordred? Arthur? Lancelot?)

  b. **Clear:** The man **that knew more about magic than any other person in Britain** didn't often sleep very well.

  (The adjective clause identifies the man as Merlin.)

  c. **Untrue:** All men knew King Arthur.

  (This is untrue because many men did not know Arthur.)

  d. **True:** All the men **who sat at the Round Table** knew King Arthur.

  (The adjective clause identifies a specific group of men that all knew Arthur. Notice the addition of the word *the* before the word *men*.)

❷ **Extra-info adjective clauses** give *extra information* about the nouns that they modify. This information is not necessary for a clear understanding of the sentence.

  a. Merlin, who knew more about magic than any other person in Britain, didn't often sleep very well.

  (The adjective clause is extra information about Merlin. There is only one Merlin in our story, so we don't need the extra information to identify him. Compare this sentence with b. in Point 1.)

b. Some historians are interested in finding out the truth about King Arthur's knights, who sat at the Round Table.

(We know that all Arthur's knights sat at the Round Table; therefore, the adjective clause gives extra information. Compare this sentence with d. in Point 1.)

❸ Extra-info adjective clauses usually modify two kinds of nouns: 1) nouns that refer to groups of people or things in general, and 2) the names of specific people, places, organizations, etc.

in general
all knights

a. Students of the Middle Ages are interested in **knights**, who often lost their lives in battle.

a person's
name

b. Merlin was very grateful to his teacher **Galapas**, who taught him most of his magic secrets.

the name of
a place

c. Merlin took the baby to **North Wales**, where he would be safe from his father's enemies.

❹ In all the examples given in Points 2 and 3 above, notice that commas set off extra-info adjective clauses, but not essential adjective clauses. In other words, if the adjective clause is necessary, commas are not. If the adjective clause is not necessary, commas are.

Activity 8   *Analyze It!*

Study each sentence. Add commas to it if the adjective clause is an extra-info adjective clause. Leave it as it is if the adjective clause is an essential adjective clause.

Examples:

Mordred who planned to become king was Arthur's nephew.

Mordred, who planned to become king, was Arthur's nephew.

The man who planned to become king was Arthur's nephew.

No commas are necessary because the adjective clause is essential to identify the man in question.

1. Guinevere who was a very sensitive person often took gifts to poor people near the castle.

2. Avalon where Arthur went to recover from injuries was very peaceful.

3. The farms that surrounded a knight's castle belonged to him.

4. The island where Arthur went to recover from injuries was a very peaceful place.

5. The woman who received notes from Lancelot hoped that her husband would never learn the truth.

6. Venison which is the meat of the deer was a popular food in the Middle Ages.

7. Ms. Chun's hobby is raising roses which are beautiful, fragrant flowers.

8. People who travel to foreign countries to study are adventurous.

9. The waiter got angry when he saw the tip my brother left him.

10. Electronic calculators which are now used by engineering students everywhere would have been considered magical by people a hundred years ago.

Point to Remember: Connectors in Extra-Info Adjective Clauses ··············

The connectors for extra-info adjective clauses are shown in the table below. Notice that the connector *that* and the zero-word Ø cannot be used in extra-info clauses.

	People	Things
Subject	1 who	2 which
Not Subject	3 whom	4 which
Others: whose, where, when		

a. Mordred, **who** came to Camelot to take over the government, was a nasty man.

b. The sword Excalibur, **which** hung over Arthur's throne, protected the king whenever he carried it.

c. Guinevere, **whom** Arthur loved with all his heart, was unfaithful to her husband.

d. The sword Excalibur, **which** Arthur carried in battle, was not a normal weapon.

e. Lancelot, **whose** love affair with the queen caused all kinds of problems, finally had to leave Camelot.

f. Camelot, **where** men and women tried to behave perfectly, was the dream of King Arthur.

g. Arthur became king at a difficult time, **when** there was no strong government in England, and knights were fighting with each other.

Activity 9   *Practice It!*

Choose ten of the sentences below, and add an extra-info adjective clause to each in the place indicated by the ^ mark. Use your knowledge and your imagination. Your resulting sentence must be original, believable, and correct. Remember the commas.

Examples:

Excalibur ^ protected Arthur in battle.

Excalibur, which was Arthur's second sword, protected him in battle.

Wild elephants ^ are often killed for their tusks.

Wild elephants, which are becoming rarer and rarer, are often killed for their tusks.

1. Guinevere ^ often tried to help people.

2. Educated Europeans of Arthur's time studied the ideas of the ancient Greeks ^ .

3. Arthur ^ had no real interest in visiting France.

4. Arthur had no real interest in visiting France ^ .

5. Merlin ^ loved cats.

6. Cats ^ were considered evil animals in the Middle Ages.

7. Guinevere often hunted with falcons ^ .

8. People love to drive European sports cars ^ .

9. Saturn ^ takes about thirty Earth years to go around the sun.

10. In the thirteenth century, Marco Polo traveled from Italy ^ to China ^ .

11. Many people want to protect the wilderness in Alaska ^ .

12. Atlantis was destroyed because its people were leading immoral lives, according to Plato ^ .

13. Belly dancing ^ is excellent exercise.

14. The Buddha ^ renounced all luxury.

15. Professional basketball players ^ often earn over a million dollars a year.

Activity 10   *Use It!*

Step 1:   This activity will give you some interesting information about your classmates. Divide into groups of three or four students. Each student in the group tells the others two interesting facts about himself or herself. These should be facts that the other people in the class do not know. (**Note:** The examples are about Katya, who is Merlin's great, great, great, great, great, great, great, great, great, great granddaughter. Katya lives in Germany and is taking an English class.)

Examples:

Katya can sleep with her eyes open.

Katya never takes elevators.

Step 2:   Combine the two facts about each student into one sentence with an essential adjective clause. Do not use the student's name. Use the word *student* instead. Write all your group's sentences—one for each student in your group—on one sheet of paper.

Example:

The student that never takes elevators can sleep with her eyes open.

Step 3:   Present your sentences to the rest of the class. They will try to guess who you are referring to.

Example:

Student 1:   (reads the sentence) *The student that never takes elevators can sleep with her eyes open.*

Student 9:   *Are you referring to Gretchen?*

Student 1:   *No, I'm not. Guess again.*

Student 6:   *Are you referring to Katya?*

Student 1:   *Yes, I am.*

Step 4:   A student from another group goes to the board and rewrites the sentence using an extra-info adjective clause and the student's name. When you finish this activity, you will have one sentence about each student on the board.

Example:

Katya, who never takes elevators, can sleep with her eyes open.

Formal and Less Formal Styles of Adjective Clauses

Points to Remember ···

❶ When adjective clauses include prepositions, there are two possible styles: formal and less formal.

   a. **Formal:**   The knight **from whom** Guinevere received love notes was supposedly her husband's best friend.

   b. **Less formal:** The knight $\left\{\begin{array}{c}\varnothing \\ \text{that} \\ \text{(whom)} \\ \text{[who]}\end{array}\right\}$ Guinevere received love notes **from** was supposedly her husband's best friend.

   c. **Formal:**   The pen **with which** Lancelot wrote the notes was made from a large goose feather.

   d. **Less formal:** The pen $\left\{\begin{array}{c}\varnothing \\ \text{that} \\ \text{(which)}\end{array}\right\}$ Lancelot wrote the notes **with** was made from a large goose feather.

   e. **Formal:**   Many people in England supported the king **on whose** throne Mordred sat.

   f. **Less formal:** Many people in England supported the king **whose** throne Mordred sat **on.**

❷ From the examples above, we can see that the preposition has two possible positions with the connectors *whom, which,* and *whose.* (**Note:** Only these three connectors can be used in the formal style.)

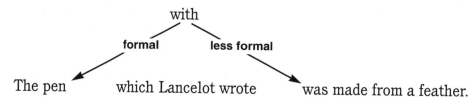

Activity 11   *Practice It!*

Step 1:   Read the information about jousting in the Middle Ages and look at the pictures.

Jousting in the Middle Ages

In the Middle Ages, two knights who had a disagreement sometimes settled it by jousting. They put on their armor,[1] took their lances,[2] and got on their horses. Starting a good distance apart, they galloped[3] their horses directly at each other. Each tried to knock the other off his horse. Many young men were seriously injured or killed.

Jousting tournaments were held to determine who the greatest knights were. The "sport" was popular, on and off,[4] from the eleventh to the sixteenth centuries in many European countries.

Step 2:   Combine the sentences in each item by changing the second sentence to an adjective clause. Use formal style only.

Example:

During the Middle Ages, there were many tournaments. Knights wore full battle armor for these tournaments.

During the Middle Ages, there were many tournaments for which knights wore full battle armor.

1. Jousting tournaments often became battles. Many young men were killed in these battles.
2. Winning a tournament was a way. A poor young man could become rich and famous in this way.
3. The knights sometimes hit each other so hard that they broke the lances. They tried to knock each other off their horses with these lances.
4. Under King Richard I, participation in a tournament was a privilege. Knights had to pay the king a high fee for this privilege.
5. Knights would sometimes joust to impress a girl. They had fallen in love with this girl.

Vocabulary

[1] armor: heavy metal clothes that protected the wearer in battle
[2] a lance: a long, pointed weapon
[3] to gallop: to ride the fastest possible way on a horse or other animal
[4] on and off: at various times

Step 3: Read the information about jousting today.

Jousting Today

A new kind of jousting tournament has been held in Mt. Solon, Virginia on the third Saturday of August every year since 1821. The tournament features[1] "ring jousting." Instead of riding at another man, a ring jouster uses his lance to catch three steel rings, which are suspended from frames over a ninety-yard track. The jouster has eight seconds to gallop his horse down the track and catch as many rings as he can with his lance.

Step 4: Combine the sentences below as you did in Step 2.

6. Modern jousters gallop down a ninety-yard track. There are three metal frames over this track.

7. They ride under the metal frames. Small rings are suspended from these frames.

8. The lances are sometimes very old. They try to spear the rings with the lances.

9. The park is well known for its interesting stone formations. The tournament is held in this park.

10. At the park, there is a small museum. Visitors can see displays about jousting in this museum.

Activity 12   *Use It!*

Jousting tournaments in Europe during the Middle Ages were a mixture of battle, sport, and ceremony. Choose one of these three topics: battle, sport, or ceremony. Write an introductory sentence telling what your topic is. Then write at least five sentences related to that topic. Include and underline a formal adjective clause in each sentence.

Example about volleyball:

I'm writing about volleyball.

1. *The net <u>over which the players hit the volleyball</u> is supposed to be seven feet, eleven inches high.*

Vocabulary

[1] to feature: to include as an important part

120

NOUN CLAUSES

PART 1

Lesson 1

Noun Clauses: The Basics

Activity 1 — Read It!

Read the following conversation between Guinevere and Lancelot. The clauses in dark letters are **noun clauses.**

Guinevere: Arthur knows something, Lance.

Lancelot: What, darling?

Guinevere: He knows **that we've been seeing each other.**

Lancelot: I'm not sure **that that's true,** but he certainly knows **that the Knights of the Round Table are upset about something.**

Guinevere: **That they're upset** is clear; they've been leaving Camelot and fighting among themselves.

Lancelot: What can we do?

Guinevere: Dear Lance, it breaks my heart to tell you **that we must stop seeing each other!** We're destroying ourselves. We're destroying Camelot, and we'll destroy Arthur!

Lancelot: Yes, we must stop. But how?

Guinevere: You must leave Camelot.

❶ A noun clause takes the place of a noun phrase or pronoun in a sentence.

a. Arthur knew
{
a fact.
noun phrase

that something was wrong.
——— noun clause ———
}

b.
{
Something
pronoun

That the knights were upset
——— noun clause ———
}
was clear.

Like nouns and pronouns, noun clauses can be in object position as in a. or in subject position as in b.

❷ Noun clauses are weak clauses. Like all other clauses, every noun clause must have a subject and a verb. In almost every noun clause, the subject is before the verb.

a. Arthur knew that **the knights were** upset.
   —— S —— V

b. Why **they were fighting** among themselves was not clear to him.
   S ——— V ———

The only exception to this rule is in sentences with *there + be*. The subject comes after the verb in these sentences.

c. Arthur could tell that there **were many problems** in Camelot.
   V ——— S ———

❸ Noun clauses can begin with *that*, a *wh-* word (or *how* or *if*), or with the zero-word, Ø.

a. **Correct:**   Guinevere and Lancelot knew **that** they had to stop seeing each other.

b. **Correct:**   Guinevere and Lancelot knew **Ø** they had to stop seeing each other.

c. **Correct:**   Arthur didn't know **why** the Knights were upset.

d. **Correct:**   The two lovers didn't know
{
if
whether
}
they could stand leaving each other.

Activity 2   *Analyze It!*

Underline the noun clause in each sentence.

Examples:

<u>That Lancelot was a courageous knight</u> had been proven many times.

Nobody knew <u>what would happen to Camelot</u>.

1. It was clear that Guinevere and Lancelot could not continue seeing each other.
2. Lancelot had already decided what he had to do.
3. Could you tell me where the castle is?
4. How quickly Lancelot could get to France depended on the speed of his horse.
5. What Mordred's goal was was his personal secret.

Activity 3   *Analyze It!*

After his conversation with Guinevere (Activity 1), Lancelot did leave Camelot for a time. He went in search of the Holy Grail. According to the fifteenth-century legend, the Holy Grail was the cup that Jesus drank from the night before he was killed. Another story from an earlier century tells how another knight, Sir Perceval, found the grail. In that story, the grail did not have religious importance; instead, it was a magical dish that never stopped filling itself with food.

Step 1: Working in groups of two or three, number the sections of Perceval's story to put them in the correct order. The first part of the story, Section A, has been numbered for you as an example.

Perceval and the Grail

Section A: _____1_____

Perceval was an innocent young man who asked too many questions. Perceval lived in the country and had never even seen a sword or jousting lance. By a strange series of events,[1] however, Perceval found himself in training to become a knight. While he was training, he proved that he was a courageous fighter and an honest gentleman. He also learned that knights should not bother people by asking too many questions. This would be impolite.

When his training was complete, Perceval decided to go out into the world, seek[2] adventure, and do good deeds.[3] He got on his horse and started traveling. After several days, he came to a great wasteland[4] that stretched far into the distance. Perceval decided to cross it.

On his second day in the wasteland, he found a great castle. The guard told him that it was the Castle of the Wounded[5] King. Because he was a knight, Perceval was invited inside and was treated as an honored guest.

Vocabulary

[1] a series of events: one thing happening after another
[2] to seek: look for
[3] a good deed: something good that people do for each other

[4] a wasteland: a poor, empty country
[5] wounded: injured

Section B: _____

She asked him if he had seen the old king with the terrible open wound in his side. When she learned that he had, she was shocked. "Didn't you ask him about his wounds?" she asked him.

"I didn't want to bother him with too many questions," Perceval said.

Shaking her head sadly, the woman told Perceval that the king had been wounded years before by an evil magician. The king's country would remain a wasteland, and his wound would remain open until a knight showed concern for him. "If you had asked about his wounds," she said, "our king would be healed, and I would have more than onions to eat."

Shocked, young Sir Perceval began to understand a new lesson. He promised to return to the castle and to undo the evil magician's terrible magic.

Section C: _____

After the meal, Perceval was given a beautiful room, and he slept very deeply. In the morning, he was astonished[6] to find himself alone in the castle. He looked everywhere, but the king, the beautiful girl, and the servants were all gone. Outside, his horse was waiting for him. He didn't know what else to do, so he got on it and started to ride away. After a few minutes, he turned around for a last look at the castle, but it had vanished.[7]

Once again, Perceval rode across the wasteland. At sunset, he came across an old woman living in an old shack.[8] The poor woman offered him an onion, which he accepted. She asked him where he had come from, and he told her about the castle.

Section D: _____

His host was the Wounded King, an old man who had a terrible cut in his side that refused to heal. Perceval was very concerned about the king's health, but he remembered that knights must not bother people with unnecessary questions. He did not ask the King about the wound.

The king's servants prepared the dining hall. A beautiful young woman brought a golden dish with an amazing variety of foods on it. What really surprised Perceval, however, was that the dish never became empty. Every time something was taken from it, new food mysteriously appeared in its place. In spite of his curiosity, however, the young knight remembered his lesson and avoided asking any questions.

Vocabulary

[6] astonished: very surprised
[7] to vanish: to disappear
[8] a shack: a small house, badly built

Step 2: Answer these questions:

1. Why was the king's land a wasteland?
2. Would Perceval have bothered the king by asking about his health?
3. How did the king stay alive in spite of his painful wound?
4. Why do you think Perceval was alone when he woke up?
5. What was the "new lesson" that Perceval learned?

Step 3: There are twenty-two weak clauses in this story: ten noun clauses (NC), five adjective clauses (AdjC), and seven adverb clauses (AdvC). (These are the only kinds of weak clauses.) In your groups, find and label as many of these as you can. The first three are done for you below as examples.

Examples:

AdjC

Perceval was an innocent young man <u>who asked too many questions</u>. Perceval lived in the country and had never even seen a sword or jousting lance. By a strange series of events, however, Perceval found himself in training to become a knight.

AdvC   NC

<u>While he was in training</u>, he proved <u>that he was a courageous fighter and an honest</u>

<u>gentleman</u>.

Lesson 2

Reported Statements and Some Other Uses of Noun Clauses

Activity 4   *Study It!*

Step 1:   Read the story below.

How Arthur Got the Sword Excalibur

After Arthur's first sword was destroyed in battle, Merlin led him to a peaceful lake. There, Arthur saw a strange sight: a graceful arm rose out of the water and held up a jeweled sword in its scabbard.[1] A beautiful lady came across the water toward him.

Lady: Arthur, I have been waiting for you. Take this boat to the middle of the lake, and you will be able to take the sword and its scabbard.

Arthur saw a boat by the edge of the water and got in. Silently, it glided to the middle of the lake. Arthur took the sword and scabbard. The arm disappeared beneath the water, and the boat silently returned to the water's edge. The lady had disappeared.

Merlin: Which do you prefer, the sword or its scabbard?

Arthur: The sword, of course!

Merlin: Then you are a fool! The sword will make you strong in battle, but as long as you wear the scabbard, you will never be injured.

Step 2:   Back in Camelot, Arthur reported the events at the lake to Guinevere. Read their conversation below.

Arthur: Guin, it was an unbelievable sight. Coming toward me, **the lady said, "Arthur, I have been waiting for you."** Then **she told me to take a boat to the middle of the lake**. I hadn't even seen the boat, but when I looked down, there it was at my feet.

Guinevere: Then what happened, Arthur?

Arthur: I got into the boat, which glided silently to the middle of the lake, where I took the sword from the arm. The boat glided back. Merlin was waiting for me, but the lady had disappeared.

Vocabulary
_____
[1] a scabbard: a cover or holder for a sword

Guinevere: I'm sure Merlin had something to say!

Arthur: **He asked me which I preferred, the sword or the scabbard.** The answer seemed obvious to me. **"The sword!" I said.**

"Then you are a fool!" he told me. I was very surprised, so I listened carefully as he explained. **He said that the sword would make me strong, but that as long as I wore the scabbard, I would never be injured.**

Step 3: Study the groups of words in dark letters. What are the two different ways that Arthur tells Guinevere about his conversations at the lake?

Points to Remember: Quoted and Reported Speech ·····················

❶ In **quoted speech,** a writer writes exactly what the speaker said, word for word. The writer puts **quotation marks** (" ") around the speaker's words. A sentence with quoted speech consists of two parts, Part 1 and Part 2. Sometimes the quotation is in Part 1, as in a. below. Sometimes the quotation is in Part 2, as in b. Notice the comma after the word "asked" in b.

——————— **Part 1** ——————— ——— **Part 2** ———
a. "Then what happened?" Guinevere asked.[1]

b. Guinevere asked, "Then what happened?"

❷ **Reported speech,** on the other hand, consists largely of noun clauses. No quotation marks are used.

a. Merlin asked Arthur **which he preferred.**

b. Arthur replied **that he preferred the sword to the scabbard.**

Activity 5   *Analyze It!*

Return to Step 2 of Activity 4. Like most people, Arthur used a mixture of quoted and reported speech to tell his wife about the conversations at the lake. Underline all examples of quoted speech <u>once</u>. Underline all examples of reported speech <u>twice</u>.

Examples:

Arthur: Guin, it was an unbelievable sight. Coming toward me, <u>the lady said, "Arthur, I have been waiting for you."</u> Then <u><u>she told me to take a boat to the middle of the lake.</u></u> I hadn't even seen the boat, but when I looked down, there it was at my feet.

---

[1] Subject and verb are sometimes reversed in this kind of sentence: "Then what happened?" **asked Guinevere.**

❶ Generally, everything inside the balloon ⬭ in a comic strip picture goes inside the quotation marks in quoted speech.

a. Merlin asked Arthur, "Which do you prefer, the sword or its scabbard?"

OR

b. "Which do you prefer, the sword or its scabbard?" Merlin asked Arthur.

c. Arthur replied, "The sword, of course!"

❷ When the quotation is in Part 1, periods are changed to commas. Compare the punctuation in a. and b. below.

———————— Part 1 ———————— Part 2 ——

a. "The sword will make you strong," Merlin said.
  comma
  not
  period

b. Merlin said, "The sword will make you strong."
  comma   period

Activity 6   Analyze It!

Parts of conversations are given below. Some are given as quoted speech, and others are given as reported speech. First, check *quoted* if the sentence is quoted speech or *reported* if it is reported. Second, if it is quoted, add correct punctuation.

Examples:

Guinevere told Lancelot that he had to leave Camelot. ☐ quoted ☑ reported

No punctuation changes are necessary.

Guinevere told Lancelot you have to leave Camelot. ☑ quoted ☐ reported

Guinevere told Lancelot, "You have to leave Camelot."

1. Lancelot told Guinevere it will be very difficult, but I will go. ☐ quoted ☐ reported

2. Lancelot told Guinevere that it would be very difficult but that he would go. ☐ quoted ☐ reported

3. At the lake, Arthur asked Merlin who is that lady. ☐ quoted ☐ reported

4. At the lake, Arthur asked Merlin who that lady was. ☐ quoted ☐ reported

5. Merlin told Arthur that she was a sorceress who would someday learn all his secrets. ☐ quoted ☐ reported

6. She is a sorceress who will someday learn all my secrets Merlin said. ☐ quoted ☐ reported

7. The club president asked the students do you know anything about African cultures. ☐ quoted ☐ reported

8. The club president asked the students whether they knew anything about African cultures. ☐ quoted ☐ reported

9. The teacher reminded her students to set their clocks forward one hour for daylight saving. ☐ quoted ☐ reported

10. The teacher reminded her students set your clocks forward one hour for daylight saving time. ☐ quoted ☐ reported

Point to Remember: A First Look at Changing Sentences to Reported Speech ··

In this lesson and in Chapter 12, you will be learning how to change several different kinds of sentences to reported speech. This will help you to learn more about noun clauses and to develop your skills with verb tenses and some other grammar points.

The four kinds of sentences that you will be working with are statements (page 130), *yes/no* questions (page 139), *wh-* questions (page 144), and commands (page 147). Each kind is changed to reported speech in a different way.

No matter what kind of sentence you are changing to reported speech, however, you must pay attention to four things:

- the tense of the verb in the strong clause (the main verb)
- the connector
- the pronouns and possessives
- the tense of the verb in the noun clause

a.

main verb
in past tense   connector

Merlin told Arthur that
his new sword would make him strong.

possessive   past focus tense[1]   pronoun

---

[1] See the table on page 131 for examples in all the past focus tenses.

b.

main verb
in past tense   connector

Merlin asked Arthur why

he wanted to marry Guinevere.

pronoun   past focus
tense

Activity 7   *Analyze It!*

Return to Activity 6. In each example of reported speech, identify the main verb, the connector, the verb in the noun clause, and pronouns and possessives in the noun clause, if any. (**Note:** One of the sentences you will analyze does not have a noun clause. Can you see why not?)

Example:

main verb   connector

Guinevere told Lancelot that he had to leave Camelot.

pronoun   verb in the noun clause

Points to Remember: Changing Statements to Reported Speech ··············

❶ The connector for reported statements is *that*.

Quoted Speech	Reported Speech
a. Merlin told the king, "You are a fool!"	b. Merlin told the king **that** he was a fool.

❷ The connector *that* can be omitted after certain common verbs like *said, told, thought,* and *believed*.

a. **Correct:** Merlin told the king **that** he was a fool.

b. **Correct:** Merlin told the king he was a fool.

❸ If the main verb is in the past tense, the verb in the noun clause must be in a past focus tense.[1]

---
[1] If the verb in the strong clause is in the present tense, the verb in the noun clause may be in any tense.

Basic Tenses in Quoted and Reported Speech

Quoted Speech	Reported Speech
a. Mordred said, "I **want** to be king."	Mordred said that he **wanted** to be king.
b. Mordred told Arthur, "The knights **are getting** more upset."	Mordred told Arthur that the knights **were getting** more upset.
c. Mordred said, "I **am going to be** king!"	Mordred said that he **was going to be** king.
d. Merlin predicted, "Someday, people **will fly** from place to place."	Merlin predicted that someday, people **would fly** from place to place.
e. Mordred said to Arthur, "I **have come** to Camelot to see you."	Mordred said to Arthur that he **had come** to Camelot to see him.
f. Mordred said, "I **have been making** friends since my arrival."	Mordred said that he **had been making** friends since his arrival.
g. Merlin told Arthur, "I **saw** the sword in a dream."	Merlin told Arthur that he **had seen** the sword in a dream.
h. Arthur said, "I **had never thought** about being king before taking the sword from the stone."	Arthur said that he **had never thought** about being king before taking the sword from the stone.
i. Guinevere said to Arthur, "You **must do** something to help the poor."	Guinevere said to Arthur that he **had to do** something to help the poor.
j. Merlin said to Arthur, "I **can help** you."	Merlin said to Arthur that he **could help** him.
k. Lancelot told Guinevere, "I $\left\{\begin{array}{l}\textbf{might}\\\textbf{may}\end{array}\right\}$ **try** to find the grail."	Lancelot told Guinevere that he **might try** to find the grail.
l. Lancelot told Arthur, "At the age of fourteen, I **could beat** any other knight in France."	Lancelot told Arthur that at the age of fourteen he $\left\{\begin{array}{c}\textbf{had been able to}\\\textbf{could}\end{array}\right\}$ **beat** any other knight in France.
m. Arthur said to the knights, "People $\left\{\begin{array}{l}\textbf{should}\\\textbf{ought to}\end{array}\right\}$ behave better."	Arthur said to the knights that people $\left\{\begin{array}{l}\textbf{should}\\\textbf{ought to}\end{array}\right\}$ behave better.
n. Arthur said to Guinevere, "I **would like** to have your opinion on something."	Arthur said to Guinevere that he **would like** to have her opinion on something.
o. Arthur said to Guinevere, "It **would be** wonderful to have a day without arguments."	Arthur said to Guinevere that it **would be** wonderful to have a day without arguments.

Activity 8   *Practice It!*

Change each statement below to reported speech. (**Note:** In some of the items, you may need to use expressions like *and that* or *but that*, as in the second example below.)

Examples:

Merlin warned Arthur, "You need to watch Mordred very carefully."

Merlin warned Arthur that he needed to watch Mordred very carefully.

Perceval said, "I would like to see the wounded king again, but I cannot find his castle." (Use *that . . . but that*)

Perceval said that he would like to see the wounded king again but that he could not find his castle.

1. Mordred's mother told him, "I've decided to send you to Camelot."
2. Merlin predicted, "In 1969, people will walk on the moon."
3. The knight told Arthur, "Your castle is strong enough to survive any attack."
4. Merlin told Arthur, "You should always take Excalibur when you travel."
5. Mordred told his friends, "Our success is going to be wonderful."
6. Mordred wrote to his mother, "I've been having a wonderful time in Camelot."
7. Mordred wrote to his mother, "Arthur puts his sword on every day."

8. The customer told the technician, "The air conditioner makes my office too cold."
9. The clerk said, "I can take a credit card instead of cash."
10. Mr. Nelson explained to Dr. Wilson, "I mailed my check, but I forgot to put a stamp on the envelope." (Use *that . . . but that*).
11. The economist explained, "A higher tax will keep people from wasting gasoline."
12. Dr. Adams explained, "I would like to fix the table myself, but I don't have time."
13. My advisor told me, "You will be on the dean's list if your GPA is 3.5 or more."
14. The dolphin told his brother, "It was fun swimming with the female human."
15. The little boy promised the little girl, "I won't pull your hair again."

Points to Remember: Time Indicators in Reported Speech ···················

1 **Time indicators** are words like *today, now, yesterday*, and *ago*. It is usually necessary to use past time indicators in reported speech because the verbs are in past focus tenses.

  a. **Quoted:**   On June 17, 1184, the boy asked the knight, "Are you going to joust **tomorrow**?"

  b. **Reported:** The boy asked the knight whether he was going to joust **the following day**.

  c. **Quoted:**   Merlin told Arthur, "I discovered my powers many years **ago**."

  d. **Reported:** Merlin told Arthur that he had discovered his powers many years **before**.

2 If a conversation took place a very short time ago, verb tenses and time indicators may not change.

A minute ago, an archaeologist was talking with his assistant. He said

he $\begin{Bmatrix} \textbf{is hoping} \\ \textbf{was hoping} \end{Bmatrix}$ to find the location of Camelot **tomorrow.**

Time Expressions of Reported Speech

Quoted Speech	Reported Speech
yesterday	the day before / the previous day
last week / month / year	the week / month / year before
	the previous week / month / year
three weeks ago	three weeks before
recently	recently
now / at the moment	then / at that time / at that moment
today / tonight	that day / that night
this week / month / year	that week / month / year
tomorrow	the next day / the following day
next week / month / year	the next week / month / year
	the following week / month / year
in three years / in a few minutes	in three years / in a few minutes
soon	soon

Activity 9   *Practice It!*

According to historian Geoffrey Ashe, there was great excitement at the monastery in Glastonbury, in the West of Britain, in the year 1190. The monks believed that they had found the tomb of King Arthur, the historical King Arthur, who probably lived from about A.D. 475 to A.D. 538.

The following letter was written by an imaginary monk, Adam, to a friend in another monastery. Change the numbered sentences to reported speech. Begin each sentence with "Adam wrote that . . ." Put the time expressions at the ends of the sentences and make all other necessary changes. Sentence a. is done for you as an example.

Example:

a. *Adam wrote that King Henry had asked them to look for King Arthur's tomb about six years before.*

> February 21, 1190
>
> Dear Malcolm,
>
> We have been having a great deal of excitement here in the last few days. (a)About six years ago, King Henry asked us to look for King Arthur's tomb. We looked all around the church but found nothing. (1)Four years ago, our church burned down. It was a terrible fire. (2)Last week, we began to rebuild the church. (3)We were digging in the ground. (4)Yesterday, the diggers found a marker under the floor. It said, "Here lies King Arthur." They continued digging. (5)This morning, they found a large coffin. When we opened it, we found the bones of a large man, and then another set of smaller bones. Near the smaller bones there were some beautiful pieces of blond hair, no doubt that of Queen Guinevere!
>
> (6)Everybody is very excited! (7)A master carpenter will soon make a beautiful double coffin for King Arthur and Queen Guinevere. (8)Next month, we are going to have a special ceremony. We will wrap the bones in silk and move them to a special place. (9)King Edward himself will attend!
>
> In the coming years, pilgrims will be able to visit the tombs. (10)I hope that you will be able to make the journey yourself some day.
>
> Yours in God,
>
> Adam

Points to Remember: Past Ideas and Beliefs ···

❶ In formal writing, it is often necessary to report past ideas and beliefs. Study the verb tenses in these sentences:

> During the Middle Ages, most Europeans **believed** that the Earth [(a)] **was** flat. They **thought** that a boat that [(b)]**came** too close to the edge of the Earth [(c)] **would fall** off into space. Educated Europeans, however, never doubted the science of the ancient Greeks, who **believed** that the Earth [(d)] **was** round.

Verbs a., b., and c. are in past focus tenses. (In c., *would* is the past of *will*.) The past focus tenses are used because these are **past beliefs**.

The same is true for d. Even though the Earth is still round today, the verb *believed* in the strong clause "controls" the tense of the verb in the noun clause. The present tense *is* would be incorrect at d.[1]

❷ The following verbs are often used in sentences expressing past ideas and beliefs.

believed	explained	learned
claimed	found out	realized
doubted	knew	thought

---

[1] At times, native speakers bend these rules about verb tenses. You can avoid mistakes, however, by following the rules. In addition, the writers of standardized tests like TOEFL expect students to know the rules of formal English.

Activity 10   *Practice It!*

Choose the best verb and put it in the best tense and voice. Use formal tenses.

> ***Examples:***
>
> Members of the Flat Earth Society still believe the Earth (be, have)
> _____*is*_____ flat.
>
> When Arthur first saw Guinevere, he realized that he (want, think)
> _____*wanted*_____ to marry her.

1. Merlin realized that Mordred (be, have) _____ dangerous to Arthur.

2. When Merlin took the baby Arthur to the home of Ector, he knew that the boy
   (be, have) _____ king someday.

3. Most historians believe that Camelot never really (exist, justify)
   _____.

4. Some students of the Arthurian legend believe that Arthur never really (create, die)
   _____. They believe that he (be, have) _____ still
   in Avalon today and that someday, when the world is ready, he (resist, return)
   _____ to be king again.

5. Some British people believe the monarchy (serve, produce) _____ a
   useful purpose in the past but that now it (be, have) _____ just a
   useless expense and should (abolish, create) _____.

6. The ancient Greeks believed that the Earth (be, have) _____ at the
   center of the universe.

7. In the sixteenth century, Polish mathematician Nicolas Copernicus developed his
   theory that the Earth (be, have) _____ one of six planets that
   (destroy, orbit) _____ the sun.

8. While cigarette advertisers no longer claim that cigarettes (have, be)
   _____ good for your health, they don't usually explain that tobacco
   products often (let, make) _____ people sick.

9. The instructor promised that the lab reports (return, develop) _____
   to the students the next day.

10. When did you learn that the moon (go, come) _____ around the
    Earth?

Activity 11 *Practice It!*

Step 1: The teacher asks Student 1 a question from the list below about Student 2.

> *Example:*
>
> **Teacher:** Chow Wei, how old is Rafael?

Step 2: If Student 1 doesn't know the answer, he or she must ask Student 2.

> *Example:*
>
> **Chow Wei:** *Rafael, how old are you?*
>
> **Rafael:** *I'm 22 years old.*

Step 3: The teacher asks Student 3 what the class now knows about Student 2.

> *Example:*
>
> **Teacher:** Ahmed, what do we now know about Rafael?
>
> **Ahmed:** *We now know that Rafael is 22 years old.*

Step 4: The teacher asks Student 4 what the class learned. Student 4 answers using the formal sequence of tenses.

> *Example:*
>
> **Teacher:** Kim, what did we find out about Rafael?
>
> **Kim:** *We found out that he was[1] 22 years old.*

1. How old is (*name*) ?
2. What language does (*name*) speak with his/her parents?
3. Where will (*name*) be at 9:30 tonight?
4. Where was (*name*) at 9:30 last night?
5. About how many people live in (*name's*) city?
6. How many brothers does (*name*) have?
7. What is (*name's*) favorite sport?
8. How does (*name*) feel about horses?
9. Where would (*name*) like to go for a perfect vacation?
10. Has (*name*) ever been to Toronto?
11. How many countries has (*name*) visited?
12. How often does (*name*) read a newspaper?

---

[1] In nonformal language, native speakers might say: "We found out that he **is** 22 years old." Using the formal tenses, however, can help you to avoid mistakes.

Activity 12 *Use It!*

Individuals' ideas change as they grow older. The ideas of the people of a country change as they become more educated and as international communication and travel increase. What about your ideas? What about the ideas of people in your country? Choose five of the general topics below, or any other interesting topics, and write a pair of sentences about each. In each pair, the first must tell a past belief, and the second must tell a present belief. (**Note:** It is not necessary to use the exact words given below. They are general topics. See the examples. The topic is "food," but the word *food* is not used in the sentences. If you want to use the word, you may, however.)

Examples:

food

When I was a little girl, I used to think that fish tasted terrible. Now I think that fish is delicious.

People in my country used to believe that tomatoes would kill them, but now they think that tomatoes are good for their health.

magic	the sky	beautiful ladies	clothes
banks	grownups	boys	girls
gallant knights	dolls	the ocean	history
good manners	horses	science	fairy tales
trucks	monster movies	teachers	doctors
husbands	wives	children	travel

Chapter 12

NOUN CLAUSES   PART 2

◇◈◻ **Lesson 1**

Reporting Yes/No *Questions*

Points to Remember •

❶ Compare these quoted and reported *yes/no* questions.

  a. **Quoted**:   The student asked the professor, "Will we ever know the truth about King Arthur?"

  Reported: The student **asked** the professor

  $\begin{Bmatrix} \textbf{if} \\ \textbf{whether} \end{Bmatrix}$ we would ever know the truth about King Arthur.

  b. **Quoted**:   The student asked the professor, "Does anybody know the location of Arthur's tomb?"

  Reported: The student **asked** the professor $\begin{Bmatrix} \textbf{if} \\ \textbf{whether} \end{Bmatrix}$ anybody knew the location of Arthur's tomb.

❷ The verb in the strong clause of a reported *yes/no* question is *ask*. The two connectors are *if* and *whether*. These connectors have the same meaning.

❸ The words *or not* can be used with *whether*, but they are not necessary.

  a. **Correct**:   The student asked the professor **whether** we would ever know the truth about King Arthur.

  b. **Correct**:   The student asked the professor **whether** we would ever know the truth about King Arthur **or not**.

  c. **Correct**:   The student asked the professor **whether or not** we would ever know the truth about King Arthur.

139

4 Every reported question includes a noun clause. The subject is before the verb in almost every noun clause. (See Point 2 on page 122.)

a. **Correct:** Arthur asked Guinevere if $\overset{\text{S}}{\text{she}}$ $\overset{\text{V}}{\textbf{loved}}$ him.

b. **Incorrect:** Arthur asked Guinevere if did she love him.

5 If the main verb is in the past tense, the verb in the noun clause must be in a past focus tense.[1]

main verb in past tense	past focus tense in noun clause

a. Arthur **asked** Guinevere if she **loved** him.

main verb in past tense	past focus tense in noun clause

b. Arthur **asked** Merlin what he **would do**.

6 Reported questions are not questions; they are reports of questions. Therefore, there is no question mark at the end of the sentence.

Activity 1   *Practice It!*

Change each *yes/no* question to reported speech.

Examples:

Arthur asked Guinevere, "Do you love me?"

Arthur asked Guinevere if she loved him.

1. Arthur asked the cook, "Do we have enough food to get through the winter?"
2. Lancelot asked Guinevere, "Will you be able to meet me tonight?"
3. Mordred asked the young knight, "Have you ever done anything right?"
4. Arthur asked the architect, "Can you design an indestructible castle?"
5. Arthur asked Guinevere, "Can you tell me your new idea for the Round Table?"
6. The head guard asked Arthur, "Do you want me to keep an eye on Mordred?"
7. Arthur asked Perceval, "Did you find the wounded king's castle again?"
8. Arthur asked himself, "Should I put Guinevere in prison?"

---

[1] See the table on page131 for examples of all the past focus tenses.

9. The man asked his friend, "Do you think Pretty Dancer will win the race tomorrow?"

10. Ratana asked Ahmad, "Does your government protect endangered animals?"

11. The server asked the customer, "Will you have some dessert?"

12. The chemist asked her assistant, "Are you going to wash that equipment today?"

13. Bill said to Jackie, "Were you able to go swimming yesterday?"

14. Donna said to Peter, "Would you like to come to a barbecue next Saturday?"

15. Sergio asked Naoki, "Do people in your country shake hands?"

Point to Remember: Reporting Short Answers ·······································

Auxiliary verbs like *did, would, had,* and *was* can be used in reporting short answers. If the main verb is in the past tense, the verb in the reported short answer must be in a past focus tense.

a. **Guinevere**: Do the townspeople have enough food?

   Woman: **No, they don't.**

   Report: Guinevere asked the woman whether the townspeople had enough food, and the woman answered **that they didn't.**

b. **Arthur**: Will you try to do the right thing at all times?

   Knights: **Yes, we will.**

   Report: When Arthur asked the knights if they would try to do the right thing at all times, they said **that they would.**

Tense Changes in Reported Short Answers

Short Answer	Report	Short Answer	Report
Yes, I am.	. . . that he/she was.	Yes, I must.	. . . that he/she must. OR . . . that he/she had to.
Yes, we are.	. . . that they were.	Yes, I should.	. . . that he/she should.
Yes, I do.	. . . that he/she did.	Yes, I did.	. . . that he/she had.
Yes, I have.	. . . that he/she had.	Yes, I had.	. . . that he/she had.
Yes, I can.	. . . that he/she could.	Yes, I was.	. . . that he/she had been.
Yes, I will.	. . . that he/she would.		

Activity 2   *Practice It!*

Make one long sentence beginning with *when* to report each of the following mini-conversations.

Example:

Arthur: Will Mordred try to take my throne next winter?

Merlin: Yes, he will.

Report: When Arthur asked Merlin whether Mordred would try to take his throne the following winter, the old man said that he would.

1. **Arthur:** Do you love me?
   Guinevere: Yes, I do.

2. **Student:** Is Arthur still in Avalon?
   Teacher: I think he is.

3. **Lancelot:** Did Merlin see us last night?
   Guinevere: I'm afraid he did.

4. **Student:** Has human nature changed since Arthur's time?
   Teacher: No, it hasn't.

5. **Arthur:** Will you marry me next spring?
   Guinevere: Yes, I will.

6. **Lancelot:** Has Guinevere received my note?
   Boy: Yes, she has.

7. **Husband:** Should we take a gift to your cousin's party tomorrow?
   Wife: Yes, we should.

8. **Passenger:** Are we going to stop soon?
   Driver: No, we aren't.

9. **Student:** Must we type our reports next week?
   Teacher: Yes, you must.

10. **Lawyer:** Did you see a tall woman talking to Ms. Lu three months ago?
    Witness: No, I didn't.

Activity 3   *Use it!*

Step 1: Work in groups of three or four students. Each group writes five interesting *yes/no* questions, each with a different auxiliary verb. Use the word *you* in each question. Write questions that you would like to ask classmates in other groups. You may want to use some of the key words below, but you don't have to.

cards	horse	dance	king / queen
thunder	fire	taxes	black magic
castle	joust	mall	bargain
ironing	injection	armor	baby sitter

Examples:

Would you like to have lived in King Arthur's England?

Do you take vitamin pills?

Step 2: Each student asks one of his or her group's questions to a member of another group, who answers it with a short answer.

Step 3: A third student makes a report of the question and answer.

Examples:

Mario: *Have you ever fallen out of a tree?*

Han: *Yes, I have.*

Hamid: *Mario asked Han whether he had ever fallen out of a tree, and Han said that he had.*

◇◇□ Lesson 2

Reporting Wh- *Questions*

Points to Remember ··

❶ Compare these quoted and reported *wh-* questions.

    a. **Quoted:**   Arthur asked Guinevere, "What did I do wrong?"

    b. **Reported:** Arthur asked Guinevere what he had done wrong.

    c. **Quoted:**   Lancelot asked Merlin, "How can I find the grail?"

    d. **Reported:** Lancelot asked Merlin how he could find the grail.

❷ The main verb in all reported *wh-* questions is *asked*. The connector is any *wh-* word, including *how, how much, how old,* etc.

❸ Every reported question contains a noun clause. Therefore, the subject is almost always before the verb.

                                              S —— V ——

    a. **Correct:**   Arthur asked Guinevere what **he had done** wrong.

    b. **Incorrect:** Arthur asked Guinevere what did he do wrong.

❹ If the main verb is in the past tense, the verb in the noun clause must be in a past focus tense.

Activity 4   *Practice It!*

Change each question to reported speech.

    Example:

    Guinevere asked Arthur, "How did Merlin learn his magic?"

    Guinevere asked Arthur how Merlin had learned his magic.

1. The little boy asked Lancelot, "How can I become a knight?"

2. The student asked the professor, "How did the legend change over the centuries?"

3. Lancelot looked in his mirror and asked, "How did I become so handsome?"

4. Guinevere said to Arthur, "Where can I get more

144

medicine for the townspeople?"

5. Kay's friend asked him, "What's it like having a king for a brother?"
6. The student asked, "Why are the early Middle Ages called the Dark Ages?"
7. Arthur asked Merlin, "What will I do after you leave?"
8. Mordred asked his mother, "How long will I have to wait to become king?"

9. The student asked the admissions officer, "What TOEFL score is required for admission into your university?"
10. The driver asked the officer, "How fast was I going?"
11. The woman asked her husband, "Why must you drive that big car?"
12. Sarah asked her captain, "How far is it to 40° North by 128° West?"
13. Marty asked the salesperson, "What kind of batteries are used in this recorder?"
14. Mack asked his roommate, "Why are you washing lights and darks together?"
15. The teacher asked the class, "Who do you think is going to win the election?"

Activity 5   *Use It!*

Step 1: Each student writes down two personal *wh-* questions to ask another student. You may

brother	pet	pet peeve	address
old	why	hobby	how much
when	where	shirt	shoes
hair	problems	favorite	how long

want to use some of the key words below, but you don't have to.
Examples:

Why don't you wear your glasses?

How much did your watch cost?

Step 2: Each student reads his or her question out loud and calls on another student to answer it. The second student politely refuses to answer the question.

Examples:

Wanna: *Why don't you wear your glasses, Fatima?*

Fatima: *I'd rather not say, if you don't mind.*

Step 3: The teacher calls on two other students to report what happened.

Examples:

Teacher: What did Wanna do, Boris?

Boris: *Wanna asked Fatima why she didn't wear her glasses.*

Teacher: And then what happened?

Toshi: *Fatima politely refused to tell Wanna why she didn't wear her glasses.*

❶ One common use of *wh-* noun clauses is **indirect questions**. Indirect questions are softer than direct questions. Indirect questions are useful when you are seeking information.

Direct question: Where is the castle?

Indirect questions: $\begin{cases}\text{I need to find out} \\ \text{I wonder} \\ \text{I wonder if you could tell me}\end{cases}$ where the castle is.

OR

Could you tell me where the castle is?[1]

❷ Native speakers mix direct and indirect questions when asking for information.

Activity 6   *Practice It!*

Student 1 changes each "hard" direct question to a "softer" indirect question. Student 2 gives a believable answer. In most cases, Student 2 will need to imagine that he or she is somebody else, for example, a teacher, a driver, or a salesperson.

Example:

When does the next bus leave for Camelot?

(Student 1 is a traveler; Student 2 is an agent at the bus station.)

Student 1:   *Could you tell me when the next bus leaves for Camelot?*
Student 2:   *Of course. The next bus for Camelot is at 2:30.*

1. What is the assignment for tomorrow?

2. How much does this shirt cost?

3. How long does it take to get to Camelot?

4. What do I have to do to become a magician?

5. When is the exam in this class?

6. Do you have any special requirements regarding homework?

7. When is the rent due every month?

8. How can I get to Westgate Shopping Center?

9. Is a research paper required for this class?

10. What do you eat on your planet?

---

[1] Normally, indirect questions do not have question marks. This example does have a question mark, however, because "Could you tell me?" is a direct question.

Activity 7   *Use It!*

Step 1: Work with a partner. Without writing, improvise a conversation in which one person is seeking information from another. Use your imagination! Use a mixture of direct and indirect questions. You may use one of the situations below or choose another.

learning to use a magical object of some kind

getting details about an assignment from a teacher

mailing a package

renting an apartment

getting information about a club from its president

finding out how to become a knight at the Round Table

Step 2: Work alone. Write out a conversation based on the one you improvised with your partner. Use a mixture of direct and indirect questions. Your dialogue must have at least five questions and answers unless your teacher gives you another minimum number.

 # Lesson 3

Reporting Commands and Requests

Points to Remember •••

❶ Compare these quoted and reported commands.

a. **Quoted:**   Mordred's mother said to her assistant, "Get me Arthur's sword, Excalibur!"

                                                    simple form

      Reported: Mordred's mother **ordered** her assistant to **get** her Arthur's sword, Excalibur.

b. **Quoted:**   Mordred told the others, "Don't try to trick me!"

                                      simple form

      Reported: Mordred **told** the others **not to try** to trick him.

❷ The main verbs for reported commands are *ordered, told,* and *commanded.* The connectors are *to* for affirmative commands and *not to* for negative commands. The simple form of the verb is used after these connectors. Notice that in the negative reported commands, the word *don't* is omitted and the word *not* is before the word *to.*

a. **Correct:**   Mordred told the others **not to** try to trick him.

b. **Incorrect:** Mordred told the others to don't trick him.

❸ The main verb for reported polite requests is *asked.* Otherwise, this structure is the same as reported commands above.

    a. **Quoted:**   The lady asked Arthur, "Could you save my mother from Sir Lakeless, an evil knight?

       Reported: The lady **asked** Arthur to save her mother from Sir Lakeless, an evil knight.[1]

    b. **Quoted:**   Arthur said to Lancelot, "Please don't bring your mirror to the Round Table."

       Reported: Arthur **asked** Lancelot not to bring his mirror to the Round Table.

Activity 8   *Practice It!*

Change the following commands and polite requests to reported speech. Use *to* or *not to* in each sentence.

Examples:

Guinevere said to her servant, "Invite all the townspeople to next week's celebration!"
Guinevere told her servant to invite all the townspeople to the next week's celebration.

Merlin said to Arthur, "Could you please pass the sugar?"
Merlin asked Arthur to pass the sugar.

1. Arthur told the servant, "Prepare my horse!"
2. Lancelot said to Guinevere, "Tell me what you think of my new hat."
3. Arthur told the knights, "Do the right thing."
4. Guinevere told Arthur, "Don't forget your sword!"
5. Guinevere said to Lancelot, "Don't smile at me when other people are around."

6. The teller said to the customer, "Endorse your check on the back."
7. The waitress said, "Please don't smoke in this part of the restaurant."
8. I said to my roommate, "Please don't let me forget my appointment tomorrow."
9. The referee told the players, "Don't push the player with the ball."
10. My mother said to me, "Eat plenty of fruits and vegetables."

---

[1] Or: The lady asked Arthur {if / whether} he could save her mother . . .

Activity 9   *Use It!*

Step 1: Each student imagines that he or she is a king or queen and writes down one affirmative instruction and one negative one.

> **Examples:**
>
> *Pay your taxes on time!*
> *Don't try to cheat the government.*

Step 2: Student 1 reads one of his or her instructions out loud. Student 2 reports what Student 1 said.

> **Example:**
>
> **Alyson:**   *Pay your taxes on time!*
> **Chang:**   *Queen Alyson told the people to pay their taxes on time.*

Points to Remember: Summary Table of Report Structures ·····················

Types	Verbs	Connectors
statements	told, said to, explained, etc.	that
yes/no questions	asked	if, whether (or not)
wh- questions	asked	*wh-* words
commands	told, ordered, commanded	to, not to
polite requests	asked	to, not to

Activity 10   *Practice It!*

Change the following sentences to reported speech. (**Note:** This activity includes all the different kinds of reported speech that you have studied.)

> **Examples:**
>
> Arthur asked Guinevere, "Do you remember meeting me the first time?"
> *Arthur asked Guinevere whether she remembered meeting him the first time.*
>
> Guinevere said to the servant, "Please prepare my horse and my falcon for the hunt."
> *Guinevere asked the servant to prepare her horse and her falcon for the hunt.*

1. Arthur asked Merlin, "Who is the empty seat for at the Round Table?"
2. Merlin answered, "It is for the perfect knight."
3. Lancelot asked his assistant, "What color shirt would go best with my eyes?"

149

4. Arthur wrote in his diary, "I must forgive Guinevere and Lancelot."

5. Guinevere said to the nun, "I have come to live with you."

6. Arthur told his servant, "Please have my horse ready tomorrow at sunrise."

7. The student said to the professor, "Who is supposed to be with Arthur in Avalon?"

8. "Avalon is the resting place for all heroes who are waiting for the right time to return to Earth," answered the professor.

9. The student said, "What is Avalon supposed to be like?"

10. "It is said to be a peaceful island on a silent lake," said the professor.

11. The agent said to the passengers, "Your plane arrived at the gate a couple of minutes ago."

12. My friend asked the clerk, "Are there any openings in married student housing?"

13. The speaker said to his audience, "Can anyone predict the future of the new technologies?"

14. The ambassador told the General Assembly, "We need to work for peace."

15. The secretary told her assistant, "Recycle all the white paper."

16. Mr. Barker asked the speaker, "How long would it take to build a tunnel from Alaska to Asia?"

17. The teacher instructed the class, "Skip lines."

18. The student asked his advisor, "Do I have to take calculus this term?"

19. Burl asked Lonnie, "Did you see that program last night about aliens from space?"

20. "I don't believe in aliens," Lonnie said to Burl.

Activity 11 *Use It!*

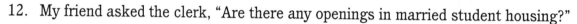

Step 1: Work with a partner. Without writing, improvise a conversation related to "Adventures at Camelot." Use your imagination! You may use one of the pairs of characters below or another pair.

Guinevere and Lancelot or Arthur

Arthur and a friend from his
    boyhood

young Lancelot and a parent

an archaeologist and an assistant

Mordred and his mother

Perceval and the Wounded King

young Guinevere and a parent

a present-day reporter
    interviewing Arthur in Avalon

the Lady of the Lake and a friend

Merlin and his teacher

Lancelot and his tailor

Ector and Arthur

Step 2: Work alone. Write out a conversation based on the one you improvised with your partner. Hand your conversation in to your teacher when you finish. Follow these guidelines as you write:

- Keep your sentences short and simple. If you write long complicated sentences, you will have problems in Step 3 when you try to change them to reported speech.

- Mix sentence types. Include at least one statement, one *yes/no* question, one *wh-* question, and one command or polite request.

- Your conversation must be at least 120 words long and must be completely original. Copy nothing from the book!

Step 3: When your teacher has checked your conversation, work alone again. Change your conversation to reported speech.

 **Lesson 4**

Noun Clauses in Subject Position

Points to Remember ··

❶ Noun clauses can begin a sentence.

  a. **That Arthur pulled the sword from the stone** surprised everyone.

  b. **Where Arthur really lived** is unknown.

❷ When a noun clause begins a sentence, it is the subject of the strong clause. That is, the weak noun clause is inside the strong clause.

sc = strong clause   *nc* = noun clause

$$S_{sc}$$
$$S_{nc} \quad V_{nc} \qquad\qquad\qquad V_{sc}$$

That **Arthur pulled** the sword from the stone **surprised** everyone.

❸ This structure is more common in formal writing than in everyday writing and speaking.

Activity 12   *Practice It!*

The Arthurian legend has fascinated people for centuries. Some things about Arthur are clear, and others are not. Answer each question with a sentence beginning with a noun clause and ending with one of the following expressions.

baffles historians	is hard to understand
is a mystery (to me)	cannot be said
is an important question	is what I want to know
is unimportant	is very clear
fascinates me	is unclear

Examples:

Where did Arthur really live?

Where Arthur really lived is unclear.

Was Arthur buried at Glastonbury?

Whether[1] or not Arthur was buried at Glastonbury baffles historians.

1. Why didn't Arthur send Lancelot away?
2. Why did Guinevere fall for Lancelot?
3. Will Arthur return someday?
4. What was Arthur's favorite vegetable?
5. Is it possible to create a perfect country?
6. Where did Merlin get his power?
7. Could Merlin really see into the twenty-first century?
8. How long did Arthur know about Lancelot and Guinevere?
9. Was Arthur a strong person?
10. Did Lancelot really wear a feather?

Point to Remember: Noun Clauses in Sentences Beginning with *It* · · · · · · · · · · · ·

Noun clauses are commonly used in sentences beginning with *it* in everyday speaking and writing. The meaning is the same as a more formal sentence beginning with a noun clause.

  a. It is likely that we will never know much about the historical Arthur.

   (= That we will never know much about the historical Arthur is likely.)

  b. It is a mystery what Arthur was really like.

   (= What Arthur was really like is a mystery.)

---

[1] Noun clauses in the subject position cannot begin with the word *if.*

Activity 13   *Practice It!*

Rewrite the following sentences. Begin each rewritten sentence with *it*. You may need to make some other changes as in the second example below.

Examples:

That historians may learn the location of Arthur's castle is exciting.

It is exciting that historians may learn the location of Arthur's castle.

Why Lancelot insisted on going to England was unclear to his parents.

It was unclear to Lancelot's parents why he insisted on going to England.

1. What Arthur would do if he returned is interesting to think about.
2. That Lancelot defeated every other knight in jousting impressed everyone.
3. That aliens gave Merlin his power is possible.
4. Why Mordred's mother wanted him to be king is unclear.
5. What caused the problems at Camelot is easy to see.
6. That Lancelot kept combing his hair in class made his teachers angry.

7. That the child took his medicine without complaining surprised his mother.
8. What kinds of problems the refugees will have in adapting to their new country is not impossible to predict.
9. Whether recording cassettes will be used in the next century is hard to say.
10. That that little dog walked over 2,000 miles to rejoin its human family thrilled everyone.

Activity 14   *Use It!*

Choose eight of the questions below. Answer each with a sentence beginning with *it* and containing a noun clause. Then rewrite the sentence beginning with the noun clause. You can use your imagination to answer questions about "Adventures at Camelot."

Example:

What did Lancelot do as a young man that made his parents proud?

It made Lancelot's parents proud that he rode a horse so well.

That Lancelot rode a horse so well made his parents proud.

1. In the story "Adventures in Camelot," what seems silly?
2. In the story "Adventures in Camelot," what seems sad?
3. In the story "Adventures in Camelot," what is unclear to you?

4. What did Merlin do that frightened people?

5. What did Lancelot do as a teenager that made his parents furious?

6. In the story "Adventures in Camelot," what doesn't make sense to you?

7. What amazes you?

8. When you were little, what made you very happy?

9. What seems unfair?

10. Once when you were discouraged, what happened that inspired you to work harder?

11. What did you do as a teenager that made your mother or father furious?

12. What did you do that made your parents proud?

Activity 15   *Use It!*

Every culture has legends and folk tales, some very complex like the story of King Arthur and the Round Table, and others very simple. Write a simple folk tale from your culture that includes conversation. Use a mixture of quoted and indirect speech in your story. Use a variety of sentence structures throughout the tale. (**Note:** A good example of how reported and quoted speech can be mixed can be found in Section B of the story of Perceval and the wounded king, in Activity 3 on page 124.)

Activity 16   *Use It!*

In this activity, you will ask a native speaker to tell you his or her ideas on an interesting topic. Then you will write a report on your interview.

Step 1:   Working in groups of three or four, choose **one** topic related to one of the two story squares in this book. Write at least eight questions about that topic that you can ask a native speaker. Write questions that will encourage your interviewee to talk. When you finish, give your questions to your teacher. (**Note:** One question is given for each topic to help you get started.)

Topics related to "A Whale of a Tale"

Aliens: "How likely do you think it is that intelligent beings exist elsewhere in the universe?"

Computers: "What do you see as the major benefits of computers?"

Endangered species: "How important is it to protect endangered species?"

Men and women in the military: "What do you think of men and women serving together in the military?"

Topics related to "Adventures at Camelot"

Utopia: "Do you think it is possible to create a perfect society?"

Chivalry: "During the Middle Ages in Europe, it was very important for knights to protect ladies. What do you think about this?"

Monarchies: If your interviewee comes from a country with a queen or a king: "What are your feelings about your queen (or king)?" If your interviewee comes from a country that does not have a king or queen: "Would you like to have a king or a queen running your country?"

History: "How can the study of history help people today?"

Step 2: Alone or in pairs, do a practice interview with a student in your class who chose a different topic from yours. (**Note:** Use your questions only as a guide. You don't have to ask all of them, nor do you have to ask them in the order that you wrote them. Let the conversation guide you. If new questions come to mind during your interview, feel free to ask them.)

To encourage your interviewee to talk more, you can say things like:

- Could you tell me more about that?

- Why do you feel that way?

- Have you always felt that way, or have your ideas changed? What made your ideas change?

- Do other members of your family feel that way too? What about your friends?

Step 3: Alone or in pairs, interview a native speaker. Choose someone who likes to talk, not someone who will just answer "yes" or "no." Record your interview. (**Note:** Your teacher will collect the recording, so be sure that your cassette fits your teacher's machine.)

Step 4: Working alone, write a report of 200 to 300 words. Begin your report by stating whom you interviewed. Then explain your interviewee's most important or most interesting ideas. Use a variety of sentence structures. You might want to use some of the following expressions in your report.

According to (*name*) . . . ,

(*Name*) believes that . . .

When I asked him/her $\begin{Bmatrix} \text{about} \\ \text{why} \\ \text{whether} \\ \text{etc.} \end{Bmatrix}$ . . . , he/she said that . . .

He/she didn't seem to want to tell me $\begin{Bmatrix} \text{about} \\ \text{why} \\ \text{whether} \\ \text{etc.} \end{Bmatrix}$ . . .

It seems strange to me that . . .

Step 5: Underline all the noun clauses in your report.

Step 6: Give your report and your cassette to your teacher.

INDEX